# BECAUSE OF OUR FATHERS

# Because of Our Fathers

*Twenty-Three Catholics*
*Tell How Their Fathers*
*Led Them to Christ*

Edited by Tyler Rowley

IGNATIUS PRESS    SAN FRANCISCO

Ignatius Press thanks Angelico Press for the permission to use an excerpt from Hanna Skandar's 2019 book *Love Is a Radiant Light: The Life and Words of Saint Charbel*.

Cover design by Kyle Rowley

To Saint Joseph

# CONTENTS

# INTRODUCTION

## by Tyler Rowley

> The family is the basis in the Lord's plan, and all the forces
> of evil aim to demolish it. Uphold your families and guard
> them against the grudges of the Evil One by the presence
> of God.
>
> —Saint Charbel

United States senator Rick Santorum had always wanted
to meet Pope John Paul II, so in the summer of 1999, he
took his family to visit the Vatican with the hope of meeting the great pontiff. They were in Rome for three days
when they finally received the call: they were invited to
the pope's private chapel for morning Mass.

At six o'clock in the morning, Rick and Karen Santorum rounded up their four young children and hur-
ried through the Vatican streets, past the Swiss Guards,
through the Bronze Doors, across two courtyards, and up
four flights of stairs to the pope's private residence. As they
stood inside the holding room, just outside the chapel,
they noticed that most of the other guests were religious
sisters, priests, and older couples. Rick and Karen, the only
guests with children, agreed that they would sit in the back
pew for the Mass to ensure they did not disrupt this special occasion. Bishop Dziwisz, the pope's secretary, was
insistent, however, that they sit in the front row. Senator

Santorum was surprised at their blatant efforts to highlight the presence of a high-ranking U.S. politician during Mass, but he agreed to their request.

Inside the chapel, they were seated so close to the pope that they could have reached out and touched his vestments. As he celebrated Mass, the Santorums were brought to tears. Never before had they seen someone so absorbed in prayer, as if he were in another world. At one point, the pope looked into the faces of their children, engaging them with his infectious smile, his face filled with joy at their presence.

After Mass in the papal residence, it is customary for attendees to meet the pope briefly. As the line was forming, the Santorums headed to the back, but, once again, Bishop Dziwisz ordered them to the front. Senator Santorum was now feeling uncomfortable for being treated so favorably because of his elected office, so he told Bishop Dziwisz that he and his family would happily go to the back of the line. Bishop Dziwisz interrupted the senator's refusal, and in his thick Polish accent said to him, "Important man."

"No, no. I am not," replied Senator Santorum.

"Important man," Dziwisz said again, this time poking his finger into the senator's chest.

Senator Santorum embarrassingly shrugged off the compliment again: "Thank you, Your Excellency, but I'm really not."

This time Bishop Dziwisz wagged his finger in the senator's face, pointed very deliberately to each of his four children, then returned his finger to Santorum's chest, and said even more forcefully, "Important man!"[1]

[1] Senator Rick Santorum, phone interview by Tyler Rowley, February 9, 2018.

It is difficult to overlook the importance of fatherhood in Catholic teaching. "Father" is the very name that Jesus gives to God; it is the title we give to priests who act in the person of Christ; and it is the father who the New Testament tells us is head of the Christian household. Perhaps the best story that underscores the importance of fatherhood comes to us from Scripture's revelation regarding the inception of the Holy Family.

The Gospel of Matthew informs us that when Saint Joseph learned of Mary's pregnancy, he decided to "send her away quietly" so as not to cause her the shame of divorce (1:19). This decision, according to the Gospel, was in keeping with Joseph's being a just and righteous man. God, however, had a different plan. He sent an angel to Joseph to calm his fears and to incorporate him into the family of the One Who would save the world from sin.

We must stop here to consider the powerful tribute to fatherhood this story provides to us. Surely, if there was ever a family who was not in need of the presence of a male figure in the household, it was this family, and yet, at the culmination of God's revelation of His love for mankind, His immediate concern is to provide Jesus with a father.

God wanted Jesus to have an earthly father because God wanted the Son to have the same kind of family that He intended for every person. Every man, and certainly every father, would do well to contemplate this divinely revealed truth. The family is God's perfectly designed human relationship that resembles His divine nature: loving and life-giving. As Pope Benedict XVI says in *Deus caritas est*, the family is "the icon of the relationship between God and his people" (no. 11). In this relationship, the father is necessary not only to create new life, but also, as exemplified by the Holy Family, to lead, protect, and educate all of the family members. As Saint Thomas Aquinas tells us, "The father is the principle of generation, of education, of learning, and of whatever pertains to the perfection of human life."[2] At the dawn of salvation, it was the birth of a child that heralded good news. That child needed a mother and a father. And if Jesus needed Joseph, how much more do you and I need our fathers?

What happens to a world that does not understand this fundamental truth about the nature of the family and the necessity of paternal care and witness? Today, a great number of men, forgetful of their divine mission, neglect their paternal role altogether, or, if they remain in their children's lives and provide for their material needs, they do not participate in their spiritual formation. Pope Pius IX, in his 1930 encyclical *Casti connubii* (*On Christian Marriage*), prophetically addressed this growing crisis:

> Christian parents must also understand that they are destined not only to propagate and preserve the human race on earth, indeed not only to educate any kind of worshippers of the true God, but children who are to become members of the Church of Christ, to raise up fellow-citizens of the Saints, and members of God's household, that the worshippers of God and Our Savior may daily increase.... For the most wise God would have failed to make sufficient provision for children that had been born, and so for the whole human race, if He had not given to those to whom He had entrusted the power and right to beget them, the power also and the right to educate them. For no one can fail to see that children are incapable of providing wholly for themselves, even in matters pertaining to their natural life, and much less in those pertaining to

[2] *Summa Theologica*, trans. Fathers of the English Dominican Province (London: Burns, Oates & Washbourne, 1922), II-II, q. 102, a. 1.

the supernatural, but require for many years to be helped, instructed, and educated by others. Now it is certain that both by the law of nature and of God this right and duty of educating their offspring belongs in the first place to those who began the work of nature by giving them birth, and they are indeed forbidden to leave unfinished this work and so expose it to certain ruin. (nos. 13, 16)

In many respects, and in many places around the world, the Catholic Church is in "ruin". Therefore, the world she is tasked with shepherding is in ruin, and this cultural breakdown can be attributed to the fathers who have abandoned their sacred duty to educate their children "to become members of the Church of Christ". This neglect leaves children unequipped to grow in virtue, pursue the world's deepest truths, worship correctly, pursue authentic justice, build healthy families of their own, and face the world in the most meaningful and impactful ways. It is true, as Pope Leo XIII pointed out over a century ago, that when children are not "enlightened by religious instruction ... every form of intellectual culture will be injurious; for young people not accustomed to respect God, will be unable to bear the restraint of a virtuous life, and never having learned to deny themselves anything, they will easily be incited to disturb the public order."[3]

The world's biggest problem is the ruin of the Catholic Church, and the Catholic Church's biggest problem is the ruin of fatherhood.

In the United States, between 2000 and 2018, at least fourteen million Catholics left the faith; parish religious education of children dropped by 35 percent; Catholic school attendance dropped by 24 percent; infant Baptism dropped

---

[3] Leo XIII, encyclical letter *Nobilissima gallorum gens* (February 8, 1884), no. 3.

by 38 percent; adult Baptism dropped by 53 percent; and sacramental Catholic marriages dropped by 45 percent.[4]

One cannot help but make the connection between this drastic decline in the practice of the faith and the great number of men who, forgetful of God's salvific plan, either entirely ignore or carelessly execute their fatherly mission to raise faithful Catholics. If the Church will succeed once again in teaching the gospel to the world, it will need to be led by fathers, who may no longer stand by as idle observers as their children are entrapped by the world and led into the destructive vices of secularism and materialism.

Now, many men and women, secular and religious, have undertaken the task of documenting the societal ills of fatherlessness. Their work is extensive and undeniable. If ever sociology yielded a conclusive truth, it is this: children suffer mightily when their fathers are absent. Speaking on this matter in *Familiaris consortio*, the Church tells us, "As experience teaches, the absence of a father causes psychological and moral imbalance."[5] The data show that every kind of societal ill from suicide to abortion skyrockets among children who are raised in households without fathers. Fatherless families may also play a significant role in making boys vulnerable to confusion about their sexual identity.[6] In his extensive scholarly work on fatherlessness,

---

[4] Center for Applied Research into the Apostolate, "Frequently Requested Church Statistics", last visited April 21, 2020, https://cara.georgetown.edu /frequently-requested-church-statistics/.

[5] Pope Saint John Paul II, apostolic exhortation *Familiaris consortio* (November 22, 1981), no. 25.

[6] See "The Psychology behind Homosexual Tendencies: Richard Fitzgibbons Makes Distinctions of Same-Sex Attractions", Zenit, December 5, 2005, https://zenit.org/articles/the-psychology-behind-homosexual-tendencies -part-1/; Joseph Nicolosi, "Fathers of Male Homosexuals: A Collective Clinical Profile", Joseph Nicolosi, M.D., last visited April 22, 2020, https:// www.josephnicolosi.com/collection/2015/5/30/fathers-of-male-homosexuals -a-collective-clinical-profile.

David Blankenship writes, "Fatherlessness is the most harmful demographic trend of this generation. It is the leading cause of declining child well-being in our society. It is also the engine driving our most urgent social problems, from crime to adolescent pregnancy to child sexual abuse to domestic violence against women."[7] The task of this book, therefore, is not to demonstrate the importance of fathers in general, but rather to show how this pivotal role of fatherhood must translate into cultivating a child's knowledge and love of God—our true Father. If paternal neglect leads to devastating natural consequences, it stands to reason that a father's religious neglect leads to devastating spiritual consequences.

Social scientists speak of biological paternity versus fatherhood. The former creates a child while the latter raises an adult. The Church wishes to speak to men about earthly fatherhood versus Christian fatherhood. The former seeks to give children all their material possessions. The latter seeks to give children a relationship with God and a vocation to serve Him. As someone once said, parents need to care more about getting their children into Heaven than getting them into Harvard. Never before in modern history have we seen so many young people declaring no religious belief (the so-called Nones). If Saint Augustine was right, and the heart is restless until it rests in God, we can be confident that the restlessness of our children today is the direct result of their lack of relationship with the God Who made them, loves them, and calls them to Himself. An earthly father is the bridge that connects his children to their Heavenly Father where the heart finds its rest.

Saint Irenaeus famously tells us that "the glory of God is man fully alive", and the second part of that quote is just

---

[7] David Blankenship, *Fatherless America* (New York: Harper Perennial, 1995), 1.

as important: "and the life of man is the vision of God."
A good father gives his children the vision of God, first
through the way he lives and loves and then through catechesis in the faith. *Familiaris consortio* continues:

> In revealing and in reliving on earth the very fatherhood
> of God (cf. Eph 3:15), a man is called upon to ensure
> the harmonious and united development of all the mem-
> bers of the family: he will perform this task by exercising
> generous responsibility for the life conceived under the
> heart of the mother, by a more solicitous commitment to
> education, a task he shares with his wife (cf. *Gaudium et
> spes*, 52), by work which is never a cause of division in the
> family but promotes its unity and stability, and by means
> of the witness he gives of an adult Christian life which
> effectively introduces the children into the living experi-
> ence of Christ and the Church. (no. 25)

A father's most important job is to provide for his children's spiritual needs. In addition to feeding them bread,
he must feed them the gospel and equip their minds with
the faith and with reasons to live a moral and sacrificial
life. A scene from the 2005 movie *Cinderella Man*, starring
Russell Crowe, provides a worthy example. Crowe plays a
supposedly washed-up boxer named James Braddock who
cannot find work to support his family during the 1930s
depression. His children are underfed, and times are getting more and more desperate. He comes home one day
to learn that his oldest son, Jay, stole some meat from the
local butcher. Braddock sharply tells the boy to pick up
the meat and follow him back to the butcher, where they
return the stolen food. Back outside on the street, the boy
expresses that he stole the food so the family could have
enough to eat and he and his siblings would not be sent
away to live with wealthier family members. The father

leans down to meet his son eye to eye and says, "Just cuz things ain't easy, that don't give you the excuse to take what's not yours, now does it? That's stealing, right? And we don't steal. No matter what happens, we don't steal. Not ever. You got me?" He then asks his son to promise that he will never steal again. "And I promise you," Braddock says, "we will never send you away." His son starts to cry. Braddock picks him up, hugs him, and says, "It's okay, kid. You got a little scared. I understand." The father carries his son home.

The meat would have nourished the boy for a night. The religious lesson, the example of sacrifice, the moral clarity, and the love of a father will nourish him for a lifetime.

This powerful fatherly influence must be cultivated daily. A good father continuously strives to grow closer to God. He loves his wife as a precious gift and bearer of his children. He falls to his knees in thanksgiving for his children and for being allowed to participate in the creation of new life. This incomprehensible blessing should give every father the deep desire to form his children emotionally, physically, mentally, morally, and especially spiritually. Through this life of love, which is assertive yet gentle, strict yet merciful, the earthly father is a living model of our Father in Heaven, and through this example, a child is introduced to God's love, and his life becomes rightly ordered.

It would be impossible to speak sufficiently of fatherhood without mentioning the Cross. It has been said that all of Christianity can be summed up in the message of the Cross. Saint Paul wrote to the Corinthians, "For I decided to know nothing among you except Jesus Christ and him crucified" (1 Cor 2:2). Saint Rose of Lima tells us, "Apart from the cross, there is no other ladder by which we may get to heaven."[8] And Saint Thomas Aquinas said: "The cross is my sure salvation.... The cross is my refuge."[9] Our modern world wishes to speak of Jesus apart from the Cross, but as the saints attest, that is impossible, just as it is impossible for fathers to lead their families apart from the Cross.

In Scripture, Saint Paul directs wives to submit to their husbands. That may surprise the average Catholic because the missalettes in our pews usually bracket that part of the reading from Ephesians as optional, and many parishes in turn skip over it. This is a travesty and injustice to families. A well-ordered family welcomes and understands Saint Paul's words. The husband *is* the head of the household. The wife *is* subject to the husband. This is a beautiful biblical lesson that we should not be ashamed to proclaim in our churches and practice in our homes. Understood correctly, the husband's headship does not mean he is given permission to dominate his wife with an iron fist. This teaching is concerned with an ordering of roles and authority that allows a marriage to function, just as authoritative ordering allows a government or business to function. The husband as the "head" means giving his wife virtuous and God-fearing leadership. This is a duty, not a privilege. It is a cross, not a crown. Saint Paul says as much in the next verse, "Husbands, love your wives, as Christ loved the church and gave himself up for her" (Eph 5:25). How did Jesus love the Church? Look to the Cross. The headship of a father is the daily acceptance of crucifixion in order to lead, protect, and sacrifice himself for his family.

[8] Quoted in *Catechism of the Catholic Church*, 2nd ed. (Vatican City: Libreria Editrice Vaticana, 2000), no. 618.
[9] Ambrose St. John, *The Raccolta*, 5th ed. (London: Burns, Oates, and Co., 1880).

For the gospel to flourish once again and for the truth of Jesus Christ to fill the hearts of men and women, fathers must reassert themselves as the spiritual leaders of their homes. A 2015 Pew study of religion in the United States found that 27 percent of Catholic adults have left the faith and an additional 13 percent identify as Catholic but largely do not practice.[10] This book is written for all Catholics, but with a sincere effort to reach the hearts of those men who make up that 13 percent. It is written for the men who, stirred by the grace of their Baptism, are still clinging to their faith, even if only by a thread. These men identify as Catholic. They attend Mass on Easter and Christmas and maybe a few other Sundays throughout the year. They have had, or will one day have, their children baptized. There is probably some sort of religious artwork in their homes. They may remember their Confirmation saint. They do not, however, go to Mass weekly. They never go to Confession. They do not pray before meals or pray much at all. They do not know what the Church teaches. And truth be told, despite their slight eagerness to have some sort of relationship with God, albeit on their own time and in their own way, they have almost no relationship with Him, and their children, unbeknownst to them, are destined to lose the faith altogether because of their example.

These men need to realize now, before it is too late, that their grandchildren will likely not be baptized or know much at all about Jesus Christ unless they take ownership of their spiritual obligations as Catholic fathers.

Let us consider for a moment that extremely sad and very realistic scenario as we address these men. First,

[10] "America's Changing Religious Landscape", Pew Research Center, last modified May 12, 2015, https://www.pewforum.org/2015/05/12/americas -changing-religious-landscape/.

ponder your ancestors. Think about the lineage of devout men that spans your ancestral tree. Your Catholic identity most likely goes back many generations—centuries, if not millennia. Now consider: Why are you letting that faith fade, not just from your family's tradition, but more importantly, from your children's lives? If your great-great-great-grandfather could speak to you, what would he say to you if he knew that you were the one responsible for the loss of the Catholic faith in the family? Better yet, what would you say to him if he asked: Why have you abandoned the faith? What have you replaced it with? Do you have a relationship with God? Do your children know anything about Jesus?

You are the beneficiary of generations of fathers who kept the Catholic faith. How tragic it would be to squander your heritage, *especially before you know what it really teaches*, and not just for yourself, but for your children and your children's children.

Truly, a father's raising his children to know and love God creates a well-functioning and sane family. The contrast of this, when fathers leave children spiritually underdeveloped, is, as we see today, familial and cultural insanity. The meaning of this "sanity" is illuminated by Frank Sheed, one of the twentieth century's most revered theologians, in arguably his greatest work, *Theology and Sanity*. Sheed makes this simple yet pivotal point about the Catholic faith:

> This book contains theology, not the great mass of it that theologians need, but the indispensable minimum that every man needs in order that he may be living mentally in the real world—which is what the word "sanity" means in my title....
>
> For the soul's full functioning, we need a Catholic intellect as well as a Catholic will. We have a Catholic will

when we love God and obey God, love the Church and obey the Church. We have a Catholic intellect when we live consciously in the presence of the realities that God through His Church has revealed. A good working test of a Catholic will is that we should do what the Church says. But for a Catholic intellect, we must also see what the Church sees. This means that when we look out upon the Universe we see the same Universe that the Church sees; and the enormous advantage of this is that the Universe the Church sees is the real Universe, because she is the Church of God. Seeing what she sees means seeing what is there. And just as loving what is good is sanctity, or the health of the will, so seeing what is there is sanity, or the health of the intellect....

Therefore if we see anything at all—ourself or some other man, or the Universe as a whole or any part of it—without at the same time seeing God holding it there, then we are seeing it all wrong. If we saw a coat hanging on a wall and did not realize that it was held there by a hook, we should not be living in the real world at all, but in some fantastic world of our own in which coats defied the law of gravity and hung on walls by their own power.... Seeing God everywhere and all things upheld by Him is not a matter of sanctity, but of plain sanity.[11]

Up until this point we have merely made the point that fathers have a unique and preeminent influence over their children's faith lives and should recognize this responsibility. That says nothing, however, about the point Sheed is making, which concerns the truth of the thing to believe. Ultimately, there is only one reason for anyone to be Catholic and raise his children Catholic: because it is true; because it is sane.

---

[11] Frank Sheed, *Theology and Sanity* (San Francisco: Ignatius Press, 1995), 7, 22–23, 25.

There are many paths that men can take to arrive at the living knowledge that Catholicism is the fullness of truth, each one speaking a different language to men whose ears are prepared by grace in different ways. Some are moved by prayer; others by repentance; others by study and spiritual reading. The cohesiveness of theology, philosophy, logic, and history attracts many truth-seeking men. There is the staggering historicity of Scripture; apostolic succession; inexplicable miracles throughout the ages; sound reasoning of the philosophers; unprecedented beauty; lives of the saints; and, of course, the life of Jesus Christ.

God, through His Church, is holding out His hand to every man. Sanity is when the man reaches back.

A rational objection to this book's aim would cast doubt on a man's willingness to do for his children what he is unwilling to do for himself. In other words, why would a father, lax and listless in his own religious life, make the effort to learn and then teach that religion to his children? A funny thing happens when a man becomes a father. Children cause men to think outside of themselves. It is because we love them so much, even more than ourselves, that we want good things for them, even if we deny those very things to ourselves. We are perfectly happy eating junk food, but we have a rule that our kids cannot eat it. We neglect sleep and study but demand healthy doses of each for our kids. It is quite a curious thing when you examine how much better we become once we have children, and we don't just want *them* to be better; we often want *ourselves* to be better *for* them.

The following story demonstrates the point: a young man sits down at a table and eats three hearty meals a day for years without once stopping to acknowledge the One Who created the food and to thank Him for bringing it to his plate. In almost robotic fashion, he consumes every calorie to keep the cogs of his body machine running. Then the man has a son. One day, he finds himself at that same table with another meal in front of him. Across the table sits his toddler, ready to devour his food as it is placed in front of him. The man stops his son. "Why don't we say a quick prayer?" says the man. "What's that?" the son replies. The man stares back, genuinely confused about how to answer. "Let's just do it, and you will see: Dear God, thank You for this food and for our many blessings. In Jesus' name we pray. Amen." The father and son proceed to eat their meal. After a few minutes, the son says, "Dad, who is Jesus?" The father says nothing but thinks, "I don't know, but I am going to find out." The child helps the father to see his own ungratefulness, and, not wanting to form that attitude in the boy, the father is moved to set a different example for his son.

Yes, parents teach children, but children illuminate the world for parents and allow them to see and come to terms with their own shortcomings as well as provide them with the incentive to seek truth and be better people. This is why you will often see parents return to church after they have children. This is a good thing, but that one act is often not an adequate example for children. Limiting the religious formation of one's family to *going to church on Sundays* is like limiting one's concern for his child's education to looking at his report card. A good father ensures that his child's education is advancing by becoming deeply involved with and attentive to his daily progress. A good father gauges his child's spiritual health in the same way. A small dose of religion that is void of substance and passion, in addition to being ineffective, can even act as a sort of inoculation to the faith, leading a child to assume there is nothing more to the spiritual life than going to a church service that he doesn't understand.

As Bishop Thomas Olmsted said, "The truth is that large numbers of Catholic men are failing to keep the promises they made at their children's baptisms—promises to bring them to Christ and to raise them in the faith of the Church."[12] In 2015, Bishop Olmsted penned a letter to Catholic men in the Diocese of Phoenix titled "Into the Breach". The bishop challenged them to stop skirting their duties as Catholic men and vigorously to protect their families from the evils of the world. He expounded:

> One of the key reasons that the Church is faltering under the attacks of Satan is that many Catholic men have not been willing to "step into the breach"—to fill this gap that lies open and vulnerable to further attack. A large number have left the faith, and many who remain "Catholic" practice the faith timidly and are only minimally committed to passing the faith on to their children. Recent research shows that large numbers of young Catholic men are leaving the faith to become "nones"—men who have no religious affiliation. The growing losses of young Catholic men will have a devastating impact on the Church in America in the coming decades, as older men pass away and young men fail to remain and marry in the Church, accelerating the losses that have already occurred.[13]

Let us now turn our attention to an unlikely source of evidence for the critical role fathers play in cultivating the faith of their children. In 1994, the Swiss government conducted a large, important study that yielded some interesting facts about "generational transmission of faith and

---

[12] Thomas J. Olmsted, "Into the Breach: An Apostolic Exhortation to Catholic Men, My Spiritual Sons in the Diocese of Phoenix", Diocese of Phoenix, September 29, 2015, https://dphx.org/into-the-breach/.

[13] Olmstead, "Into the Breach".

religious values". (The full title of the study is *The Demographic Characteristics of the Linguistic and Religious Groups in Switzerland*.) This study offers empirical confirmation of the philosophical and theological teachings of the Church on the topic of fatherhood.

The study divided fathers and mothers into three categories based on their attendance of church services: (1) regular, (2) irregular, and (3) nonpracticing. It divided the adult children of the parents into the same three groups.

The results of the study were quite telling, although, from a Catholic perspective, not surprising.

When the father and mother are regular churchgoers:
- 33 percent of their children are regular.
- 41 percent of their children are irregular.
- 26 percent of their children are nonpracticing.

The following results indicate what happens when the father is a less faithful churchgoer than the mother:

When the father is an irregular churchgoer and the mother is a regular churchgoer:
- 3 percent of their children are regular.
- 59 percent of their children are irregular.
- 38 percent of their children are nonpracticing.

When the father is nonpracticing and the mother is a regular churchgoer:
- 2 percent of their children are regular.
- 37 percent of their children are irregular.
- 60 percent of their children are nonpracticing.

Now let's see the numbers when Dad is a more faithful churchgoer than Mom:

When the father is a regular churchgoer and the mother is irregular:
- 38 percent of their children are regular.
- 38 percent of their children are irregular.
- 25 percent of their children are nonpracticing.

When the father is a regular churchgoer and the mother is nonpracticing:
- 44 percent of their children are regular.
- 22 percent of their children are irregular.
- 33 percent of their children are nonpracticing.[14]

In summary, if fathers fall away from or are lax in their commitment to the faith, their children have only a 2 to 3 percent chance of going to church regularly when they are adults. On the other hand, if dads go to church regularly, no matter how devoted moms are, between 38 and 44 percent of their children will grow up to be regular churchgoers and between 66 and 75 percent will go to church at least occasionally (regular and irregular). The study concludes: "It is the religious practice of the father of the family that, above all, determines the future attendance at or absence from church of the children."

Simply put: evangelize fathers, evangelize the world.

Ultimately, this issue is serious not for the sake of maintaining some family tradition. That's not why Catholicism matters. We are dealing with the eternal destiny of every person's soul, which depends on how each person lives the one life that God has given him. How we live will determine how we die, and there is no one more responsible for the salvation or damnation of a soul after death than a father.

[14] Council of Europe, European Population Committee, *The Demographic Characteristics of the Linguistic and Religious Groups in Switzerland* (2000), 38.

This fact calls for a paradigm shift in the mind of many Church leaders. Consider how many resources are dedicated to educating our youth in the faith. Quite a lot of time, talent, and treasure is spent on youth groups, CCD programs, and schooling. But if these kids go back home to the witness of a father who has all but lost the faith, their future relationship with Christ and His Church is essentially a foregone conclusion. If we do not evangelize the dad, the kids will likely be lost. This sort of approach to passing on the faith seems contradictory, but as Catholic author and apologist Eric Sammons explains, it is "the Biblical method of salvation".

In the Bible, whenever God works with a group of people, He does not direct His energies toward the entire group, but toward a mediator. Think of Abraham, Moses, or David: each of these men represented a much larger group of people. God first influenced and converted the one man, then He allowed that individual to influence the group he led and represented. This is also the fundamental way in which the Catholic Church operates: we have bishops and priests who receive specific graces and powers that are then used to help the laity draw closer to Christ. The father is the mediator—the "priest"—of the family, the domestic church. Therefore it makes sense, both sociologically and theologically, to focus on fathers in order to save the children.[15]

When I was introduced to the aforementioned Swiss study, I immediately started to think about all the people in my life, trying to see if its conclusion held true for the people I know. One by one, I went through my friends and acquaintances, and almost without exception, I could

---

[15] Eric Sammons, "No Church for Young Men", *Crisis Magazine*, January 9, 2020, https://www.crisismagazine.com/2020/no-church-for-young-men.

trace a person's dead faith to his nonpracticing father. Conversely, everyone I knew with a strong faith had a father who was serious about the faith. This dynamic persisted with each new person I met. Whenever I encountered a fallen-away Catholic, I would ask about his father. The response was inevitably along these lines: "My father doesn't go to church. My mother is religious, but my father isn't."

Then, one morning, I was listening to Catholic radio. Father Gerald Murray of the Archdiocese of New York was discussing his recently deceased father. Father Murray told a poignant story that captured my attention. One morning, a seven-year-old Gerald Murray realized that his dad attended daily Mass. Shocked, he pointed out to his father that Catholics have to go to Mass only on Sundays. His dad replied that he enjoyed going to Mass every day because he loved receiving Jesus in the Eucharist. Father Murray identified this as a pivotal event in his life: the moment when he first realized that the strongest and best man in his life lived in humble and dedicated service to God.

As I was driving and listening to this testimony, it became evident that Father Murray's Christian life, including his priestly vocation, was due to his father's example. It reminded me of a similar story that Patrick Madrid, a prominent Catholic apologist, often tells about his father. As a teenager, Patrick was dating a Protestant girl whose father would routinely challenge his Catholic faith and show him all the ways Catholicism contradicted the teachings of Scripture. Patrick, young and outmatched by the older man, told his own father about his troubles with his interlocutor. His father was calm and confident as he grabbed a book from the family library and helped his son research the answers. To this day, Patrick will tell you that his zeal for the faith blossomed once he encountered his father's love for Christ and the Church.

It was undeniable. Everywhere I looked, I saw the strong witness of a father behind the faith of a serious Catholic.

Pope Saint John Paul II was intimately aware of the power of a father's witness. On the occasion the fiftieth anniversary of his ordination to the priesthood, he spoke about the many influences he had during his early life that led him to a life committed to serving God and others:

> My preparation for the priesthood in the seminary was in a certain sense preceded by the preparation I received in my family, thanks to the life and example of my parents. Above all I am grateful to my father, who became a widower at an early age. I had not yet made my First Holy Communion when I lost my mother: I was barely nine years old.... After her death and, later, the death of my older brother, I was left alone with my father, a deeply religious man. Day after day I was able to observe the austere way in which he lived. By profession he was a soldier and, after my mother's death, his life became one of constant prayer. Sometimes I would wake up during the night and find my father on his knees, just as I would always see him kneeling in the parish church. We never spoke about a vocation to the priesthood, but his example was in a way my first seminary, a kind of domestic seminary.[16]

So many years later, it is not surprising that, as the successor of Saint Peter, he felt so passionately about underscoring a different father in his private chapel, not because of his job as a United States senator, but because of his vocation as a father and the powerful influence he has on his children.

---

[16] Pope John Paul II, *Gift and Mystery* (New York: Doubleday, 1999), 20.

I decided to see just how common this trend of faithful fathers influencing their children to practice the Catholic faith was. I contacted men and women across the country whom I knew to be serious, committed Catholics and asked them about their fathers. This book was born from those phone conversations as, one by one, I discovered that all of them not only had amazing fatherly examples but were also eager to share their stories and tell how their fathers led them to Christ.

## Acknowledgments

*A special mention of gratitude to my father James Rowley, my grandfathers Henry Rowley and Edmond Petit, and my many great-grandfathers who persevered and kept the Catholic faith down through the centuries. I know the gospel because of these fathers.*

# John Castillo

*John Castillo lives with his wife, Maria, near Denver, Colorado, and works as an engineer. In 2019, his eighteen-year-old son, Kendrick, charged at a gunman in his high school classroom, dying in the act. All other students were saved. John has become an advocate for treating school shootings as domestic terrorism. He manages a Facebook group dedicated to Kendrick and his advocacy, "In Honor of a Hero: Kendrick Castillo".*

Let me start out by saying that on May 7, 2019, when my son, Kendrick, laid down his life as a martyr, he was not only a hero; he was also my best friend and the love of his mother's life.

On that day, one of two shooters entered Kendrick's classroom and drew a gun on twenty-eight students. Kendrick rushed at him and pinned him against a wall, which led to the shooter's being subdued—but not before our only son lost his life to the lone bullet the gunman was able to fire.

To understand how Kendrick became this fine young man, you have to understand the incredible influence that my father, Kendrick's grandfather, had on my life.

Salvador Castillo was born and raised in northern New Mexico in a small farming community with his brothers and sisters. At the age of four, he suffered the loss of his father (my grandfather) to a sudden heart attack. Shortly after, his older brothers went off to fight in the Second World War, and the rest of the family moved to Denver, Colorado. Even though my grandmother remarried, my father never had a strong father figure in his life, so when the opportunity to join the United States Marines presented itself, he jumped at the chance and ended up serving his country in the Korean War.

When my father returned home from the war, he married my mother and started the family he had always wanted for himself. We were a strong Catholic family. My father made sure we always attended Mass and respected the teachings of the Church. I have many memories of getting up on Sunday morning as a young boy and watching my father shave in the bathroom before he dressed us in our suits for Mass. I specifically recall those Sunday morning lessons of how to tie a necktie. On those mornings, it was clear just from the way we dressed that the Mass was something special, very special, and that our Catholic faith was something to be proud of.

When I was old enough, I became an altar server. I was the first boy to sign up. Serving the Church and the community brought me great joy and made my father proud.

My father showed me how to pray. At meals. At bedtime. And most importantly, in the Rosary. That prayer has never left me, and now more than ever I continue to rely on its promises: "now and at the hour of our death".

As I grew into a young adult, I loved going to church and helping in the community. After Maria and I got married, we continued to embrace our Catholic faith and serve the Church. When the time came for Maria and me to have children, we were very excited. Maria became pregnant and we were so happy, but we suffered a miscarriage. As time went on, we worried that we might not be able to have children. But then Maria became pregnant with Kendrick.

Kendrick's birth changed our lives in such a wonderful way. When he was conceived, Maria and I knew what a gift we had received from God. I remember how happy we were when the time came to have our only son baptized and to introduce him to Christ and His Church.

I loved Kendrick so much. I love him still. I spent so much time with him, and I truly embraced every second of it. I always feared that I would lose my son, not to his death, but to my own, due to a heart condition I have. This made me cherish every single second I spent with Kendrick. We went camping. We went fishing. We hunted deer and elk in the high Rockies of Colorado. And we went to Mass. Maria and I taught Kendrick the faith in the same way that I had been taught. I was reliving with Kendrick the life I had with my father, and this is the beauty of having a strong father figure in one's life: with each generation, everything is made new again.

The time had come for Maria and me to make a decision about Kendrick's schooling. We enrolled him at Notre Dame Catholic School, where he stayed from prekindergarten to eighth grade. It was a great choice. Kendrick was an altar server and helped the priests with funerals. He took great joy in helping people, and because he was involved in so many things, he was very well liked by the community. Kendrick participated in science fairs, was a DJ at school dances, and even played Jesus in the school play. He helped the Knights of Columbus at their parent-teacher pancake breakfast every year. On weekends, we went to the four o'clock Saturday Mass, where I would usher. It did not take long before Kendrick started coming back and standing with me, and before I knew it, he was the youngest usher, sporting the smallest red usher's jacket. All the people at the Vigil Mass loved seeing him. He was a youthful, vibrant sign of hope with a smile as big as his heart.

One particular Saturday afternoon in December, it was snowing in true Colorado style. It was so bad outside that I was surprised to see an elderly woman coming into the church. I told her how impressed I was by her commitment to get to Mass that night. She told me that seeing Kendrick was her motivation, that seeing my son brought her joy. She explained what a blessing he was to her, how she waited all week to see him. That conversation meant so much to me. It was maybe the first time I really understood how special my son was. I saw that he wasn't just a blessing to my wife and me, but rather his life touched so many people.

I am a Knight, a member of Knights of Columbus Council 4844 in southwest Denver. Kendrick was too young, of course, to belong to the Knights, but that did not stop him from participating in pretty much everything we did to help raise funds for those in need. Tootsie Roll drives. Picnics. Holiday gatherings. Kendrick helped with it all. The guys loved him. Oftentimes Kendrick would listen to the veterans tell war stories. Kendrick was so impressed with their patriotism and service to our country, along with their strong faith. It was truly a blessing to have such brave men of character surrounding my son.

Kendrick's grandfather was also a big part of his life. Every October when the leaves started to fall and the first snow was getting ready to sweep in, the three of us would get together for our annual elk-hunting trip in the Rocky Mountains. That trip meant so much to us. It was a time for three generations of Castillos to bond and spend time together in the beautiful outdoors around a campfire. My father would tell Kendrick about his experiences in the Korean War, along with many other stories from a time that seemed undeniably better. My father taught Kendrick how to start a fire and track animals. We would laugh and have a lot of fun. My father and I started taking Kendrick on these trips when he was just three years old, and we never missed a year until my son lost his life in 2019.

My life had so much purpose in raising Kendrick and giving him the experiences and the good life that my father had given me. There were times when my wife would call me at work, ask if I was very busy, and tell me that I should take some time to grab a Happy Meal and go eat lunch with Kendrick. I would always take her up on the suggestion and show up unexpectedly at school. I will never forget those times. That type of stuff is so important. Sometimes we need to stop doing what has become the social norm—what some people might think is important, like making as much money as we can or gathering material things that in the end have such little importance compared to the love we show our family. We should take more time to thank God for the life and blessings He has given us and then enjoy these blessings in simple ways whenever possible. For some reason, I think God gave me the grace to understand this lesson well while Kendrick was with us. I spent so much time with him and his friends working on cars, mentoring his high school robotics team, going on school and church retreats. These things helped build up Kendrick into the type of man who would sacrifice himself for others. They gave me a lifetime of memories with my son, who had to leave way too soon. Thank you, God.

I know that this is a story about fatherhood, but I must tell you about my wife, Maria. She is the one who gave Kendrick his amazing heart. Maria has always loved children, and when Kendrick was born, he became her everything. When he was a baby, she would do all the things mothers do with their children—dress him in nice clothes, teach him to talk, read him books, put on videos like

VeggieTales—and I was always in awe of how joyful she was in caring for Kendrick. My son possessed that same joy in life. Maria's bond with Kendrick was quite special, and she also played a major role in teaching Kendrick about his Catholic faith. Cooking was one of their favorite hobbies. They would prepare meals in the kitchen together, usually making Kendrick's favorite dishes. When Kendrick grew older, he would invite his friends over, and Maria would cook meals for all of the kids, knowing it made Kendrick feel special. And anything that made Kendrick happy made Maria happy. Maria would always sacrifice the "finer things" in life in order to give more of herself to Kendrick. She is so selfless. She would plan all of our vacations—to places like Legoland and Sea World—so that our son would have the best possible childhood. At robotics competitions and other school events, she always contributed whatever she could, bringing food for everyone to enjoy. When Kendrick began learning to drive, Maria would take him out and teach him traffic safety before I got home from work.

Our lives, especially Maria's, have changed in a significant way since Kendrick died. It will never be the same. During the court proceedings against the shooters, Maria gave her testimony and stated that her life was over. There was not a dry eye in the courtroom that day. Every morning, Maria walks through the house and kisses photos that we have of Kendrick, and then every afternoon we drive to the cemetery. To be perfectly honest, the hardest part for me has been to see my wife's pain. I just pray that I am strong enough to carry us both through this life until the day we meet Kendrick again.

The special bond I shared with Kendrick sometimes makes me think of the two gunmen and their fathers. What if those young men—let's call them Shooter A and

Shooter B—had been raised by honorable men like my father? Shooter A regularly witnessed his father beating his mother, when his father was around at all. Most of the time, this man was absent, running drugs from Mexico to the States. Eventually he was deported for domestic violence and gun charges. Just eleven days before the attack, Shooter A tweeted that he missed his father. In fact, Shooter A was not a "he" at all, but rather a biological female who "transitioned" in high school to living as a male. Truly, a father can make or break his children. As for Shooter B, I know he was adopted. Before leaving his house to kill his classmates, he spray-painted "F—Society", "666", and a pentagram in his garage, then doused his mother's car with gasoline and set it on fire. I can't say for sure, but I suspect there were no father-son fishing trips or discussions about God's love in that home.

I was not surprised when I learned about what Kendrick did. His whole life led up to that moment. It's a funny thing. On the one hand, I am so proud of him for being that man. On the other, it's hard not to wish he had been a little less virtuous so that he could still be with us. Help me, O Lord, to trust in your ways.

You can probably see that Kendrick absorbed all the good things he and I had been raised with, all that he had been taught by strong and faithful Catholic men, positive father figures who loved God. In one split second, Kendrick summoned up all he had learned in his life in order to protect his friends and save their lives.

Kendrick was doing what his grandfather, father, mother, and Church taught him. He was being like Jesus. He was doing what Jesus had done for all of us so many years ago on that small hill in Jerusalem. And there is no greater love than that.

2

# Bishop Joseph Strickland

*Bishop Joseph Strickland is currently the bishop of the diocese of Tyler, Texas. He attended Holy Trinity Seminary and the University of Dallas, earning his bachelor's in philosophy in 1981. He received a master of divinity degree in 1985 and was ordained to the priesthood for the diocese of Dallas that same year. Upon the elevation of the diocese of Tyler in 1987, he became a member of its newly formed presbyterate. He received his licentiate in canon law in May 1994 and shortly after was named rector of the Cathedral of the Immaculate Conception in Tyler. He was ordained the fourth bishop of Tyler on November 28, 2012.*

My father, Raymond E. Strickland, was born in 1921 and grew up a Southern Baptist near the town of Clarksville, Texas. Like many of his contemporaries, he joined the armed forces shortly after the bombing of Pearl Harbor in 1941. He entered the Navy just shy of his twentieth birthday and was ultimately assigned to a destroyer tender named the *Dobbin*. He found himself in Sydney, Australia, where he met my mother, Monica Hart, an Irish Catholic who grew up in the suburb of North Strathfield. I was born in Fredericksburg, Texas, on October 31, 1958, the sixth of seven children. Around the time I was born, my father became Catholic, and thus began the story of another Catholic father who would have a significant impact on the faith of his children.

As I remember, my father fully embraced the faith that he adopted through the influence of his Catholic wife. I would describe his relationship with the Church as being very solid and committed, always relying on my strongly catechized mother for the finer points. He demonstrated an unwavering commitment to the Church and a deep respect for the priests who served our small mission church of Saint Catherine of Siena. He was an intelligent man and occasionally found himself at odds with his still-Protestant family, including his mother. I remember one episode as a kid in which I overheard my father trying to explain the Catholic approach to Scripture and my grand-mother exclaiming, "Don't start attacking my Bible!" This scene represents the ongoing clash that took place between the Catholic family of which my father was the proud head and his Protestant family who would never understand his new faith, the faith of his wife and chil-dren. The skirmishes did get heated at times, but never to the point of an overt rupture in the family. When I was ordained a priest, my father told me how proud he was of me, and I suppose that is music to the ears of any young man. We all want to please our fathers, and I was no different. Meanwhile, my grandmother attended my ordination to the priesthood and almost got expelled from her church for it.

My parents had their share of struggles in their mar-riage and in raising a family of six children. One son died in infancy, and then they lost another when he was just eighteen. I suppose one of the strongest lessons I learned from both my parents was that whatever we were facing, we could always turn to our Catholic faith for strength and support. I will not idealize my relationship with my father. There were some real challenges and conflicts, especially through my teenage years. But as I look back now from a more mature vantage point, I appreciate my father much more.

While I was in the seminary, my relationship with my father grew significantly, and we were blessed with a true mutual respect. I believe my studies and formation for the priesthood helped me to focus on the most important things in life, and when it came to those important things, my father was a rock. He certainly had his faults—a bad temper, which often caused deep hurts in his wife and children—but when it came to the most important elements of being a man, being an American, and being a Catholic, my father was a true role model. He never was very successful financially, and I realize now that much of this lack of success was rooted in a solid integrity that was always ready to speak up when injustice raised its ugly head. Those traits didn't win him a lot of points with his bosses, but I feel sure that they won him significant points when he stood before the Lord at the end of his life. One common scenario for all of us Strickland children was the following: one of us would make some sort of mistake or do something bad that another kid had done, and then we would commit the error of responding to my father's inquiry with "But I didn't think ..." He would immediately pounce on that phrase, often with a good dollop of anger, and say quite correctly, "That's just it—you didn't think." I admit I never really learned to find another way to respond to my father's questions, no matter how many times I stepped into the "I didn't think" trap.

One of the hallmarks of our family was that we were raised to be proud that we were Catholic and to recognize that being Catholic was the best gift we had, the greatest blessing any person or family could have. My father's faith was not something he spoke of much as we were growing up. Certainly, occasional questions arose as the family navigated the 1960s and '70s, but my father's primary impact on my life regarding the faith was in the way he lived rather than a lot of direct discussion or teaching of Catholic doctrine. We lived in a rural setting on one hundred acres of farm land just outside of Atlanta, Texas, only a couple of hours' drive from where my father was born. I would not describe our family as poor, and food was always abundant, but we were not among the well-to-do of our small community.

We have always shared the family story that whenever the family moved from one town to another, my mother's first question was "Is there a church?" There was never any doubt as to what kind of church my mother was asking about. It went without saying that she was asking if there was a Catholic church. In East Texas, there are many churches, but in the early 1960s Catholic churches were few and far between. When the family began to prepare to move to the hundred-acre farm where I grew up, my mother posed her inevitable question, and my father's somewhat clever response was "There will be!" The reality was that in 1963 in the small town of Atlanta, Texas, there was no Catholic church, and I believe it is reasonable to say that the residents of the town would have been quite happy for that to remain the case.

According to family record, my father quickly went about the business of fulfilling his promise to my mother that there would be a Catholic church in Atlanta, Texas. My father's deep devotion to my mother was always an inspiration to me as a boy growing up, and surely this devotion was a major part of his inspiration regarding his efforts to see that a Catholic community was available to the family. I would also have to say that my father knew that he would have no peace until my mother had a nearby Catholic church where she could raise her family in the faith that she always described as "the greatest treasure a person could have".

My father reached out to a handful of other Catholics in the area, and they contacted the bishop of the diocese of Dallas, which included Atlanta at the time. Even a group of enthusiastic Catholics weren't able to convince Bishop Thomas K. Gorman to establish a new mission, but they did manage to convince him to allow Glenmary Home Missioners to begin to develop a Catholic presence in Cass County. My earliest memories of attending Mass as a child come from the Atlanta City Hall, where we began having Mass offered by the Glenmary priests. As a six-year-old child, I didn't realize that it wasn't the usual practice to fold up the altar and put it in storage after Sunday Mass was over. I can say with confidence that I am a bishop of the Catholic Church now due in no small part to my father's determination to make good on his promise that there would be a Catholic church in Atlanta, Texas. Saint Catherine of Siena Parish still serves the people of Cass County thanks to a Baptist boy who became Catholic.

3

# Anthony Esolen

*Anthony Esolen is a professor and writer in residence at Magdalen College in Warner, New Hampshire. He has written roughly twenty-five books, including a three-volume translation of Dante's* Divine Comedy *(Random House) and, most recently,* Nostalgia: Going Home in a Homeless World *(Gateway Editions) and* The Hundredfold: Songs for the Lord *(Ignatius Press).*

It was December 1977. I was a freshman at Princeton, going to Sunday Mass now and then. I knew only one other Catholic who attended Mass, and there was something heavy and grim about the services in the yawning Gothic chapel on campus, late on Sunday afternoon. I was falling prey to spiritual pride and sloth.

Meanwhile, my father was sitting against a tree in the snow, in the middle of the woods, with his hunting rifle at his side. "I thought I would never get up again," he told me.

He was only forty-three, but the arteries in his heart were hardly squeezing any blood at all. He might have died right then. A couple of months later, the surgeon operated—a triple bypass, which was a fairly new procedure in those days. I visited my father in the hospital, and he lay in bed, white as a sheet, utterly helpless. I was stunned. In my confident youth, I took for granted what he told us before he went under the knife. He told us not to worry; he would be fine. That was my father's way. I never saw him worry. It wasn't that he was devil-may-care; quite the contrary. He was a pillar of responsibility. But he did not worry.

Worrying was pointless, but there was more to it than that. It was one of the ways my father protected us. If he said, "We'll be all right", we could bank on it, and he would go about his business, making sure to give us no reason for concern. But now that his life was at stake, something else came to the fore, something besides stalwart common sense and protective love for his family. That was his faith.

Dad's father would rather drink whiskey than go to Mass. His neck had been broken in an explosion in the coal mines, and that was the end of his days making a miner's wages. It was also the end of his days without pain. He took to drink to dull the edge. Dad went to church with Grandma and his three brothers and six sisters. Some of my aunts and uncles persevered in the faith, and some didn't. But my father—he was the son whom Grandma set aside in her heart to become a priest. That was also the hope of Father McNeill, whom my father served as an altar boy for a long time. Dad was somewhat shy, gentle of speech, a hard worker, very intelligent, and exceptionally good looking. He didn't have that vocation to the priesthood. He met my mother on a double date, back in the time when boys and girls liked one another and had a lot of innocent fun together. My mother came from a staunch Catholic family too—one in which there was never a drop of alcohol. The two fell in love instantly.

I am the oldest of four children in my family. Some of my earliest memories are of the Mass. I was too small to see the priest; his voice seemed to be coming from the great vault of Saint Thomas Aquinas Church, its ceiling covered

with paintings I did not understand. I am just old enough
to recall the Latin: *Dominus vobiscum. Et cum spiritu tuo.*
On Sunday we always went to Mass. It was unthinkable
not to. As I got a little older, I became aware that there
were some people who didn't, but that was bad; there was
something wrong with them, something missing.

We wore our best clothes to Mass. That meant a coat
and tie for me, and a clean shirt and pants. It also meant
shining my shoes, and to this day the smell of shoe polish
will in a moment make me a small boy again, squeezing out the liquid and buffing the shoes with a brush. It
was the right and ordinary thing to do. When we got to
church, we sat on the right-hand side, with my father taking his place on the aisle, my mother beside him, and the
children in a row to her right, however many of us there
were at the time. There was no crawling over the pews,
or munching on cookies, or flipping the pages of color-
ing books. It never occurred to us that somebody would
do those things in church. My little brother, a bundle of
energy, would sometimes get a little fidgety, but my father
would glance at him sidelong, and that would be that.
It wasn't that Dad was so strict. He spanked me once or
twice that I remember, when I was small, but he didn't
ever get really angry, he never raised his voice, and he
certainly didn't care very much about small infractions.
He had authority, and that was why he hardly ever needed
to show it. It was in his person.

Mass might be over, but Sunday wasn't. Here is something hard to explain to people now. When I grew up,
most businesses were closed on Sunday. Restaurants were
an exception, and a couple of gas stations. Sunday was for
piety in two ways. You gave honor to God, and then you
gave honor to the family. On Sunday, without fail, we
went to visit Dad's mother and father, who lived three

miles away. (My grandparents on my mother's side lived across the street.) We'd stay there all afternoon, and have supper, always macaroni and meatballs. Very often, some aunts and uncles and cousins would be there too, and the children then had to take their plates and sit on the staircase, two and two, all the way up.

This wasn't just a habit for Dad. It was the thing to do. After Grandma and Grandpa died, the families of my aunts and uncles began to grow a little more distant, and so my father sought to bring them all back together every summer, including great-aunts and great-uncles and their children and children's children.

We didn't *talk* about the faith back then, because so much of it was self-evident to us; and my parents, the children of coal miners, owned but a handful of books, along with a Douay-Rheims-Challoner Bible and the *World Book Encyclopedia*. We lived the faith. My parents took it for granted that their children would attend the Catholic school in town, even though neither of them had done so. They took it for granted that we would attend one of the diocesan high schools. The first break in that tradition came when I went to Princeton—where I did stumble into an excellent education, though it was a place, as I've since said, where faith and reason go to die.

That reticence was over when my father came out of the operating room. He had to quit smoking. He did, cold turkey. He had to give up his bottles of beer. He did, completely. He had to give up a lot of his favorite foods. No problem. And he grew more serious about his Catholic faith. He joined the Cursillo movement. He volunteered at the church, as a lector, a member of the choir, and a helper at the annual fund-raising picnic. He began to read books about the faith. All of this was going on in his soul. I thought it was very good, but it was distant from me, not to my taste; meaning that I was young and took myself and my opinions too seriously.

The surgery was a success. But several years later, Dad was diagnosed with colon cancer. That, too, he played down, so that when he had his operation in 1983, I was blithely unaware of how serious the condition was. The cancer would get the better of him at last. He died in 1991, at home. The family was there. We knew it would be his last day, because he could no longer drink. When his breathing grew difficult, we huddled round him, and he whispered his last words to my mother with his eyes wide open: "I love you."

"Well done, good and faithful servant!" I said at his funeral, in a short eulogy. I didn't know at that time that eulogies aren't proper for a funeral Mass, and of course I was presuming that Dad had been taken up into glory, without the need for Purgatory. He himself wouldn't have thought so. But he had always been a very good and strong man, and in the years since his brush with death in those snowy woods, he had become a deeply pious and holy man.

My father died during my first year as a professor at Providence College. I had not yet written any articles or books from a Catholic point of view. My wife and I were married in 1986, and we had a little girl whose only memory of my father is that he would sit in his favorite chair, and he was ill. I had no idea, when he died, what his loss would mean to me. I suddenly felt the shock of fatherlessness; there was no longer that pillar, that rock. Later on, I would tell my friends that what I really needed was an abbot: a spiritual father who would give me direction, someone reliable, whom it would be an honor to obey.

I think it goes without saying that if it weren't for Dad, I might very well be that proud and spiritually dusty man that my life at Princeton was training me to be: a man without faith or hope or charity, but instead a show of confidence, some natural kindness, and despair. In a human sense, I owe my father all that I am. That doesn't mean that I have no similar debt to my mother or to my wife. The pillar holds up the roof, but a home or a church is not just a pillar. Still, I think that without the good Father McNeill, my father would not have become the man he was, and without my father, I would not be writing these words now.

My last male ancestor, an uncle, died a year ago. I feel all the closer to Dad. I think about him all the time and remember him and my aunts and uncles in prayer each night. I hope he would be proud of me. I know from experience what one word of affirmation from a father can mean. And though it may still be presumptuous of me, I will say it again for him: "Well done, good and faithful servant!"

4

# Alexandra DeSanctis

*Alexandra DeSanctis is a staff writer at* National Review, *where she publishes reporting and commentary. Her work focuses on U.S. politics and culture, elections, abortion policy, and the pro-life movement. She cohosts the* For Life *podcast at the* National Review. *She has been invited to several colleges to speak on conservative activism, the pro-life movement, and succeeding in journalism as a young writer. Prior to becoming a staff writer, Alexandra was a William F. Buckley Jr. Fellow in political journalism with the National Review Institute. She is a 2016 graduate of the University of Notre Dame, where she studied political science, theology, and the U.S. Constitution. Her work has been published in the* Wall Street Journal, *the* Atlantic, *the* Washington Examiner, *and the* Human Life Review. *Find her on Twitter at @xan_desanctis.*

My father has always had a special devotion to Joseph, the husband of Mary, since he is the saint for whom my father was named. I remember my father coming home from work, when I was in grade school, on the evening of May 1 with a loaf of Italian bread, a surprise to celebrate the feast of Saint Joseph the Worker. From when I was very young, I have had a devotion to the saint too. But, at least initially, my love for him stemmed almost entirely from the fact that my father loved him first.

That story is a simple way to articulate how deeply and significantly my father's example has affected my spiritual understanding and led me to place my Catholic faith at the center of my life. I believe because I saw him believe first. I am faithful, even in the midst of scandal, because he is faithful, though it is difficult for both of us, in different ways, I imagine.

I remember learning as a child that none of the words of Saint Joseph are recorded anywhere in the Bible, and this disturbed me for quite some time. I wished that the Gospel writers had thought to tell us even a word or two that he had said, so that I could understand him better. I wanted to commit something to memory, latch on to something that would give me more insight into the only member of the Holy Family who ever sinned.

But as I grew up listening to the same Gospel stories time and again in church and at home, I realized that Joseph's role in the salvation story is no less powerful just because his words aren't recorded in Scripture. He has a profound effect even in his profound silence—and, I think, *because* of his silence.

We are forced to focus on him not as a man with wise words to impart but as a man of deep thought and, most of all, a man of action. We see that he is a righteous man who accepts the will of God, even when it makes no sense in human terms. We see how well he set aside his all-too-human fears and dedicated his life to the immense task of giving the love of an earthly father to the Son of God.

Like the Joseph of the Gospel, my father is a man of few words—but he is a man of deep thought, one who has taught me more with his actions than any words could communicate. As a result of the way he has lived, he has had a profound effect on my life and my faith.

My father grew up in Canfield, Ohio, the younger of two children, and his parents both had been born to men and women who had immigrated to the United States in the early twentieth century from southern Italy. He had the blessing of a large extended family, all of whom lived in the Youngstown area, and he grew up with all the benefits of that sort of close community. His childhood instilled in him a love for home and for family, always evident to me in his desire to be present for my younger brother and me when we were children—not because he felt that he must be, but because he wanted to be.

When my father was in high school, his own father was diagnosed with cancer and passed away within two years, another formative experience that I believe led my father to want to spend as much time with us as possible and to spend that time well. For most of my life, my father has been a lawyer in private practice, but despite the demands of his profession, he chose to be home as often as he could, prioritizing family life over the worldly accolades that he could have attained from reaching the pinnacle of his profession. He would rather have been with us—and he so often was.

Though he always worked hard, he thought it was equally important to make time for his family. He was there for nearly every one of my brother's Little League games, and he sat through every one of my ballet recitals (although I'm told he sometimes fell asleep during the parts I wasn't in). When he spent a few years traveling to and from Providence, Rhode Island, for business, we often went with him, staying a week at a time in a hotel as my mom homeschooled us, so we could be together as a family. He made sure that he—that we—would always prioritize the things that mattered most.

The older I get, the more I realize that my father chose to be a lawyer not out of ambition, but for us, so that we would be able to have the type of life he thought would be best for us, so we wouldn't have to worry about having a good home, or clothes, or food. He viewed his career not as a means of personal satisfaction or glorification but as a means of providing for my brother and me the sort of education that would increase our knowledge and our ability to pursue our goals—and an education that would help us understand and internalize our Catholic faith. Though he loved history and writing, and likely would have been happy and fulfilled working as a professor, he placed his desire for our best interests above his own.

In large part because of those choices my father made, my mother was able to stay home with my brother and me, even homeschooling us for several years, which was an immense blessing that enabled me to grow in my faith from a very young age. Later, I attended a Catholic school that instilled in me a deeper understanding of what it means to be Catholic—an understanding that explains how, as an adult, I freely choose to retain and practice the faith into which I was born. That understanding informs my personal life and my work today and leads me to view my career not as a pursuit of ambition but as an answer to a call.

It was also in large part because of my father's hard work—and, more important, because of his constant belief that I could accomplish whatever I was called to do—that I was accepted to Notre Dame. My time there was one of the greatest blessings of my life. The friendships I developed with both my peers and my professors, as well as the occasions to deepen my Catholic faith, were transformative. Without those years and relationships at Notre Dame, I don't think I would have found such quick success pursuing my vocation in journalism.

It is because of my father, too, that I have committed the early part of my career to pro-life reporting and commentary.

When I was born, in the mid-1990s, my father was working on Capitol Hill for Senator Mike DeWine from Ohio. DeWine was one of the most pro-life members of the U.S. Senate, and my father worked for him on the Senate Judiciary Committee. He was handling much of the senator's work on abortion policy, especially the controversial Republican effort to pass a ban on partial-birth abortion, that heinous, medically unnecessary, late-term abortion procedure.

This past year, as I was writing a speech to deliver on a college campus, I decided to go back and watch some of DeWine's speeches from the debate in the 1990s over the partial-birth abortion ban. I wanted to understand it better for my reporting on abortion policy, and I wanted to learn more about the man for whom my father had worked. As I sat at my desk watching a video of DeWine defending the ban on the Senate floor in November 1995, the camera panned to the side for a moment, and I caught a glimpse of the face of the man seated beside the senator.

It was my father.

I watched the rest of DeWine's remarks with tears in my eyes. I had known for some time, of course, about my father's work in Congress and his involvement in the pro-life cause. Both of my parents had raised me to care deeply for the unborn, and they taught me from an early age how much this issue matters and gave me the tools to come to my own passionate stance against abortion.

But in that moment, unexpectedly seeing my father on film, I realized that he had taken his belief in the sacredness of life, his belief in the value and dignity of the unborn, and had done something about it. He had dedicated part of his life to helping write the words that a politician would speak on the floor of the U.S. Senate in opposition to state-licensed killing of the most innocent among us. He had contributed to what eventually would be a successful effort to prohibit a procedure that takes the life of a partially delivered infant in an unspeakably brutal way.

I realized, as I watched DeWine, how deeply my father's choices have shaped my own beliefs, the way I see the world, and the causes to which I have committed my life. And I felt in that moment, for the first time and in a transformative way, that I had been born with the seeds of the pro-life movement in my heart. I have that heart, in large part, because of my father.

When I was in middle school, I was riding with my dad to Mass one Sunday morning. I don't remember how the subject came up, but he told me a story about a time he had gone to a Protestant church service with a friend. The service was perfectly fine, he told me, and he knew they all sincerely believed in the same God he did. But he said, too, that after that experience, he knew he could never think about leaving our Church. He had looked around the room where they had worshipped, and, in the end, saw only what was missing: there was no tabernacle. Though their church was full of faith, it was empty of that which matters above all.

Today, as our Church faces a uniquely challenging moment in its long history of challenges, and even as my heart is torn by the knowledge of abuse and corruption rooted so deep within it, I remember that story. I center my Catholic faith not in the men who direct His Body, but in Christ's Body given for us—in the ultimate value and transcendent reality of the Eucharist.

My belief in that truth above all sustains me. I retain my faith in it in no small part because of the witness of my father, who taught me by his example to believe in the only thing that really matters.

I am not and never have been a Catholic because of the flawed leaders of the Church or the sinful men and women who sit in its pews. Though his influence on my life is undeniable, my father is not, in the end, the reason I'm Catholic. Like my father—whose steady presence and witness taught me to believe in the faithfulness of God—I am Catholic because I have the gift of faith that we belong to Christ's Church, that the Good Shepherd leads it still, and that He will lead us home, if we let Him.

# 5

# Patrick Madrid

*Patrick Madrid is an author, theology professor, and host of* The Patrick Madrid Show, *heard daily on the Relevant Radio network. A very well-respected apologist for the Catholic faith, Patrick has participated in many formal debates against leading scholars ranging from Protestant to atheist; these debates can be found on the Internet. Patrick and his wife, Nancy, have eleven children and twenty-five grandchildren.*

"My dad can beat up your dad!" is a taunt most little boys will at some point shout at a rival. This is because fathers are archetypes of masculinity. They image to their children—for better or for worse—what it means to be a man, a dad, a husband, a protector, and a provider. And children learn lessons from their fathers—for better or for worse—that remain imprinted on them for life. It happened to me.

As I survey the circuitous path of life I've traveled thus far, not always knowing where I was headed, though always aware of where I had started, it's clear that many of the decisions I made along the way—the causes I came to espouse, attitudes I adopted, mistakes I made, and successes I met with—were in some way or another the result of lessons I learned from my father, Bernard E. Madrid. Born in El Paso in 1937, the third of six children, he grew up speaking only Spanish in a devoutly Catholic Mexican family whose members had, in the 1920s, been forced to flee their haciendas, factories, and government jobs in Mexico when the revolutionary reign of anti-Catholic terror became overwhelming. My paternal grandmother, Esperanza, recounted stories about how desperately bad things were in Mexico when she was young. Once, Pancho Villa and his gang descended on her home in search of her father, a judge in the town of Camargo, one hundred miles south of Chihuahua. Providentially, my great grandfather caught wind of the raid just in time to don some peasant clothes, clamber onto a burro, and hightail it out into the desert, where he waited for Villa and his men to leave, after they had loitered for a couple of days, intending (unsuccessfully) to shoot my grandfather when he returned. My grandmother told me thrilling stories of the heroic young Jesuit martyr Father Miguel Pro, who carried out a clandestine priestly ministry in Mexico City, always wearing disguises, successfully eluding the authorities who frantically searched for him for two years before finally capturing and executing him by firing squad. My dad heard those same true stories of heroic Catholicism as he grew up, and I believe they had the same effect on him as they did on me. He passed on to me an ardent love for the Catholic faith, a deep knowledge of its teachings, and a keen awareness of the danger and suffering sometimes occasioned by being a faithful Catholic in the midst of persecution.

Several of my earliest memories of my dad are from 1963, when I was three; memories of him tossing me playfully into the air, catching me, as fathers do, and laughing loudly as I whooped and hollered with glee, a father-son duet of closeness; memories of riding me around on his back in the small yard of our duplex in Monrovia, California. Those and all the other fun and funny moments I can recall of him from back then when he was a young man are a trove of colorful, if faded, post-cards from my childhood.

One stark early memory is of what happened on November 24 of that year, two days after President Kennedy was assassinated. I don't remember anything about the assassination itself, other than a few vague flashbacks of seeing my parents crying and distressed (I had never seen my dad cry) and another fleeting memory of being with them in church as they prayed with many other people who were also crying and distraught. What I do remember vividly, almost photographically, is sitting next to my dad on the couch in our living room and seeing a man get shot to death on live TV. My dad and I and everyone else in the country who happened to be in front of the TV at that moment watched in horrified disbelief as Lee Oswald, Kennedy's assassin, was gunned down by Jack Ruby while being led in handcuffs through the parking garage of the Dallas Police headquarters. I didn't understand what was happening and was startled when my dad leapt to his feet and started freaking out, shouting agitatedly. As an adult, I asked him about that day, wondering what he remembered of it. He confirmed the details of my mental image of the event and described his shock and anger that the man who killed the president had taken his secrets to the grave.

Another memory I still see like a photograph in my mind: I'm about three, standing in the doorway of the bathroom in our modest home, watching my dad shave. He's wearing a white T-shirt and slacks and is leaning toward the mirror, his face lathered in Burma-Shave. Passing the razor across his face, he talks to me, and I to him, though about what, I'm not sure. This visual echo from my past is suffused with the impression that my dad was telling me that someday I, too, would grow up to be a man and that I, too, would shave. That such a mundane and easily forgettable vignette—shaving—could become an iconic memory of that long-ago father-son moment fascinates and puzzles me. Why then? Why that? It is the mystery of memories. All I know is that this particular interaction with my dad, for some reason, made an impression on me that hasn't dimmed with the passage of time. It was a life lesson about life itself, how time passes and things change and how we're all heading toward a goal. Ultimately, that goal is God Himself. The profound mystery of the great *exitus-reditus* (leaving and returning) of life and being and of all God's creatures, who come from Him and return to Him, was ever so slightly unveiled before me that day I watched my father shave. His simple words about growing up were, as I reflect on them now, a faint tracing of the arc of being that reaches toward our final fulfillment in eternity.

There was something casually heroic and debonair about my father, especially as a young man. Back when he was in his mid-twenties, not long out of the military and at the peak of his physical perfections, his wavy, jet-black hair, broad smile of straight, white teeth, taut physique, and bulging biceps made him seem like a coiled steel spring. And though I never saw it happen, I'm quite sure he could have gone *mano a mano* with any other dad and won. In this, my dad was a paradigm of manhood for me—a protector, provider, and leader.

Once, when I was eight, Mr. Morrison from across the street showed up at our home around midnight, drunk and belligerent, banging on the front door and shouting nonsense. Rather than calling the cops and waiting for them to handle things, my dad bravely opened the door and confronted the six-foot-three 230-pound bruiser. Then he physically barred him from barging into our home.

Wild-eyed and gesticulating violently, the booze-addled man demanded to see "your wife and kids!" He kept trying to push past my father but couldn't because my father faced him down, grappling with him, until he had forced him off our porch and away from our house. Seeing that he wasn't going to get past my dad, our disturbed neighbor wandered off into the darkness, shouting incoherencies. That lesson in bravery was very important to me.

I remember that my dad spanked me a lot when I was a kid (or so it seems), though that really says more about me than about him. I was a mischievous kid and pretty much deserved every spanking I got—as well as those I didn't get because my parents weren't always wise to my misbehavior. I don't carry any grudges about getting spanked, grounded, and otherwise punished for my misdeeds while I was growing up.

Looking back, I see many lessons in justice in my dad's firm hand when meting out punishments. I also remember the many second chances he granted me, even when I didn't deserve them. Those lessons about justice and mercy—not from what my dad said, but from what he did and didn't do—enabled me to pursue a similar course with my own children, trying to instill in them a deep sense of God's love for us as the foundation of both His love and His mercy. As Jesus said, quoting Hosea 6:6, "Go and learn what this means, 'I desire mercy, and not sacrifice.' For I came not to call the righteous, but sinners" (Mt 9:13).

As life wore on and my dad began to shoulder more and more of the cares that riding herd on a big family (I'm the oldest of eight) can pile on, I remember being dimly aware of how complicated and pressurized his life sometimes became. His job as an electronics engineer paid enough to make ends meet, but not much more. We had a comfortable home, though we lived simply, and I can't recall ever going hungry, but we ate very basic, humble food because that was pretty much all we could afford on my dad's paycheck. No-frills dinners of Hamburger Helper, or a plate of beans and rice, or, of course, a cheap and easy meal of tostadas or bean burritos were all very common at Casa Madrid; this was never a problem for me because I love Mexican food.

But the frugality my dad exercised in our family budget contained other important lessons beyond how to get the most out of a dollar. I will never forget the sense of shock and admiration I felt when I was in seventh or eighth grade and my mom explained to me that the reason my dad's wingtip shoes he wore every day to work had a nickel-sized hole clear through each sole was that he preferred to wear worn-out shoes so that there would be enough money for her to buy shoes for us kids. My dad sacrificed for us, really and truly, though he never said anything about it. Many times, I can remember eating a hasty breakfast with my siblings before heading off to school and there being just enough milk in the fridge for us kids to have cereal. It never occurred to me, until my mother explained it, that my dad often skipped breakfast before work, not because he wasn't hungry, but because there wasn't enough food for him and us to eat our morning meal. You see, it was the little things, the quiet and unspoken things, he did that made the biggest impression on me.

So many of the lessons my dad taught me were unspoken, in fact. He showed me by his life. For example, I've never in my life heard him utter a swear word—not when some maniac cut him off in traffic; not when someone spoke harshly to him, or when I disobeyed him, or when some misfortune popped up; not even when he hit his thumb with a hammer while working in the garage would he ever use profanity. Oh sure, my dad could get angry, even furious, with people and situations (not being perfect and needing God's grace to make up for our short-comings was another important lesson he imparted to me by word and example), but he never swore or cursed.

And the powerful thing, for me, is that I don't recall him ever sitting down and lecturing me on the importance of avoiding foul language. He just showed me by the way he lived. When I experimented briefly with profanity in high school, mainly because some of the other kids used it regularly (and I wanted to fit in), I soon realized how lame it was to talk like that and quickly dropped it like the bad habit it could easily have become, were it not for my dad's good example. It was then, I can see now, that I developed a positive horror of blasphemy. Hearing others take God's name in vain was and still is an occasion of sad-ness and revulsion for me. I owe that to my dad. And I'm grateful for that lesson. Purity of speech may not be the most important thing in life, but it is important and reveals something about the inner person. My dad taught me by example that a true gentleman doesn't debase himself and those around him with profanity. "And he called the peo-ple to him and said to them, 'Hear and understand: not what goes into the mouth defiles a man, but what comes out of the mouth, this defiles a man'" (Mt 15:10–11).

The English word "hero" derives from the Latin *heros*, often used to refer to the demigods of ancient Greece and Rome. In time, it came to mean someone of extraordinary talent or character. And it is in this sense that my father has been my hero. He's not a perfect man, of course—only Jesus is—but over his long life, with its ups and downs, tragedies and triumphs, and all the hidden little mun-dane details in between that make up a lifetime, my father nonetheless reflected to me the image of God the Father, who is the sum of all perfections. I don't idolize my dad, which would be both myopic and futile, for, as he taught me, idols obscure God from our view and separate us from Him. Rather, my dad has been for me an icon of what it means to be a man, a father, a husband. In his own imperfections and limitations, he showed me what it means for God's grace to build on my nature.

# 6

# Jesse Romero

*Jesse Romero is a full-time bilingual Catholic lay evangelist, who is nationally acclaimed for his dynamic, upbeat Christ-centered preaching. A resident of California and a retired Los Angeles deputy sheriff, he is a devoted husband and father. Jesse has a bachelor's degree from Mount St. Mary's College in Los Angeles and a master's degree in Catholic theology from Franciscan University of Steubenville in Ohio. He shared his reconversion story in the book* Catholics Wake Up *(Servant Books) and authored* Lord, Prepare My Hands for Battle, *a Catholic men's manual on spiritual warfare. As a speaker, Jesse has the ability to take the sometimes-complex teachings of the faith and make them understandable with his straight-talk approach. Jesse hosts two daily radio programs through Virgin Most Powerful Radio (vmpr.org).*

My dad beat up a rapist after Mass.

It was 1969 and I was eight years old. We had just left the Sierra Mexican Restaurant in San Fernando, California. The memory has been burned in my heart. It was a "sheepdog training moment" for me in masculine virtue at an early age. It was an example of chivalry and courage, an image that would form me as a Catholic man throughout the course of my life.

Here is what happened: my parents won a prize at our annual parish fiesta (carnival)—Santa Rosa Catholic Church in San Fernando. This is where I was born and raised along with my three brothers and my sister. The prize they won was a hundred-dollar gift certificate to this nice Mexican restaurant. That was a lot of money in 1969.

We attended the 3:00 P.M. Holy Mass on Sunday as a family, as we did every Sunday. My parents were active in the parish. My dad was a lector and an usher; my mother cooked meals for the priests once a week and ironed their albs and cassocks. I witnessed the love my parents had for the priests and our church. After Holy Mass, we drove to Sierra's Restaurant for dinner with our hundred-dollar gift certificate. The five Romero kids were elated; we had never been to a sit-down restaurant with waiters, candles, dim lights, and mariachi music. This was the first time we had been to such a restaurant as a family. My father led us in grace before the meal, and we ate to our hearts' content.

It was after 5:00 P.M. when we all walked to the car through the back door of the restaurant, which led to an alley, which led to the parking lot. As we exited the restaurant and stepped into the alley, I saw a woman inside a parked car in the alley. She was screaming, and on her back was a large man punching her and trying to tear her clothes off. She was kicking the windows of the car and screaming, "Help me, help me, get off me, get off me, help me, help me!"

I stared at the stunning scene in disbelief. I wanted to help her. I felt this anger in my heart, but what was a nine-year-old with pipe-stem arms going to do against this hulking grown man? I looked around in a state of panic and wondered who was going to help this lady. Suddenly, I saw my father take off his tie and run over to the car. I looked at my brothers with my eyes wide open and said: "Dad's gonna get in a fight!" My dad told my mom to go back inside the restaurant with us kids and call the police. The only one who followed my mom was my sister. The four of us boys stood there and saw Dad rush the car, open the back door, and jump on the back of the attacker, trying to pull him off. My dad was about five foot eleven, 215 pounds, and the attacker was considerably bigger. My dad was yelling at him to let her go, and he had to punch him several times in the back of the head in order to get him to loosen his grip on the victim, who was on her back with half her clothes ripped off. My dad softened him up with punches and then put the suspect in a rear headlock. My dad forcibly pulled him out of the car and had him controlled. The police pulled up in a patrol car and the victim began telling the police in a loud, frantic voice that the suspect beat her and was trying to rape her. Then she told the police that my father had intervened and saved her. The police took the suspect from my father and placed him under arrest. There were other witnesses in the alley who told the police the same thing. The police ran the suspect for wants and warrants and discovered that he was wanted for a string of rapes in the San Fernando Valley. My mother and sister came out of the restaurant and stood next to my dad and were told by the police that this man was a serial rapist who was on the Los Angeles Police Department's most-wanted list.

I noticed that there were at least six other men who had stepped out into the alley on their way to their vehicles that afternoon. They all saw a woman being beaten in a car and having her clothes ripped off, and they all ran to their cars in fear. Many of them had wives or girlfriends with them as well. As I saw them running, I thought, "Why are these men running? This lady needs help. Why don't all these men stop him together?" While my father saw these men running away from this crime in progress, he rushed toward a violent confrontation. That was pure courage.

On the way home, we asked our dad, "Were you afraid?" My dad reminded us that we had just come from Holy Mass. "I had Jesus with me; the other guy didn't." My father used this moment to catechize the family on the drive back home. He told us that because of the graces and prayers of the Mass and because of his relationship with God, he was not afraid of this younger, bigger, violent criminal. His faith gave him fortitude.

At the young age of eight, I now had a newfound respect for my Catholic faith.

I already had a good relationship with my father, but that day, he became my hero. No Marvel Comics Avenger could ever take his place. My dad was also my hero because I saw him practicing his Catholic faith. I saw him praying the Rosary often with my mom. Before I got married, he had the courage to have a man-to-man talk with me. He bluntly told me that he had been faithful to my mom throughout their marriage and that I was expected to be a good and faithful husband. Talk about raising the bar. But that's what a young man needs to hear from his father.

I know where my dad found the courage to do what other men did not attempt to do. It's because my dad's hero is God. "For a child is born to us, a son is given to us; / upon his shoulder dominion rests. They name him Wonder-Counselor, God-Hero, / Father-Forever, Prince of Peace. / His dominion is vast / and forever peaceful, / Upon David's throne, and over his kingdom, / which he confirms and sustains / By judgment and justice, both now and forever" (Is 9:5–6, NABRE).

My eulogy for my father was brief:

Dad—we do not grieve like the nonbelievers who have no hope. We did not lose you at the moment of death;

we lost you when you entered the Church at the day of your Baptism. From that day on, you belonged to God—Psalm 22:10. Throughout your illness you embraced your cross, you entered the school of suffering without complaining, and you offered up your sufferings to the Lord daily. Throughout your entire bout with cancer you never lost the joy of being Catholic. Dad, you have taught me several important life lessons—to love God, live in a state of grace, save souls by sharing our faith. Cancer destroyed your body, but it never touched your soul. Rest in peace, pray for me, and I will pray for you until I see you once again in the Promised Land.

My wife, Anita, eulogized my father:

Saint Augustine said, "If you pray well, you will live well; if you live well, you will die well; if you die well, all will be well." You are now well, in the land of the living. You were the best father-in-law one could ask for. You were a righteous man of great faith, a great example to my husband and children. Isaiah 3:10 says, "Tell the righteous that it shall be well with them." Death carried you home to God, where you truly belong. Rest in peace, Dad. Amen.

7

# Father Paul Scalia

*Father Paul Scalia is a priest of the Catholic Diocese of Arlington. He studied theology at the Pontifical Gregorian University and the Pontifical University of Saint Thomas Aquinas in Rome. Ordained in 1996, he is now episcopal vicar for clergy and pastor of Saint James Parish in Falls Church, Virginia. He has written for various publications and is a frequent speaker on matters of faith and doctrine. Father Scalia is author of* That Nothing May Be Lost: Reflections on Catholic Doctrine and Devotion *(Ignatius Press, 2017) and editor of* Sermons in Times of Crisis: Twelve Homilies to Stir Your Soul *(Saint Benedict Press, 2019). He is the son of the late Supreme Court justice Antonin Scalia.*

Pope Saint John Paul II visited Chicago in April of 1979. We lived in Hyde Park at the time, right off the University of Chicago campus. My parents arranged for us to go to the papal Mass in Grant Park. They sent my older brothers on ahead to stake out a place for the rest of us. Even with that advance team, however, we still found ourselves way in the back of the enormous crowd. I was only eight years old and remember almost nothing about the Mass. Indeed, the little I recall has more to do with my own father than the Holy Father.

At some point during the Mass, my father lifted me up and seated me on his shoulders. Needless to say, not the sort of thing he typically did at Mass. He then handed me his expensive opera glasses, which had been pressed into service as binoculars that day. Thus situated, I could see the pope. Despite my vantage point, he was still just a white blur far away. But that didn't matter. The important thing was that Dad had put me on his shoulders and let me, a clumsy eight-year-old boy, use his fancy glasses.

That memory has been with me for years. Now, in light of my father's death and of my own spiritual fatherhood, I see it as an apt image of what my father gave me.

First, identity. The reason we were in Grant Park in the first place was that we were a particular kind of people. Our friends in school and from the neighborhood were not there. We were there because we were different. We were Catholic, and that meant that certain things were just part of life: Mass, Confession, grace before meals (no matter how rapidly), priests over for dinner, the hasty Hail Mary as we began a long drive, and going to see the pope on a cold spring day in Chicago.

We also knew we were different because there were so many of us. It is hard for a family with nine children to blend in. We rarely encountered families as large as ours. It was only later that I made the connection. We were not just a large family that happened to be Catholic; we were a large family *because* we were Catholic. We were a big family because Catholicism meant something to Mom and Dad, and that something was worth being different.

"Why would you want to be like everyone else?" More than one of us heard that question from our father, typically in response to the child's contention, "Everyone else is ..." Always delivered with an incredulous look, it admitted no response. It communicated the absurdity of wanting to be like everyone else and, by extension, the blessing of having a distinct identity. Of course, this was not the trivial "being your own person" (whatever that means). It was, rather, the identity that faith and family bestowed upon us.

"We have heard with our ears, O God, our fathers have told us" (Ps 44:1). The psalmist means the story of how the Lord delivered the Hebrews from Egypt and formed them into the nation of Israel—how He gave them an identity distinct from all other nations. It was the Jewish father's duty to hand down that story and identity to his children.

Fatherhood is always caught up with bestowing an identity on one's children. The identity we receive from Mom is organic and instinctive. The identity from Dad must be more deliberately given—and received. Patrimony indicates the inheritance of wisdom and knowledge that we receive from our ancestors. It gives us an identity and keeps us from being historical orphans, isolated in our own little blip of time. The word "patrimony" comes from the Latin *patris* and *munus*—"the father's duty". It is indeed his duty to give his children an identity so that they know their place in the world.

My father also gave me clarity. During the papal Mass we attended, my father put me on his shoulders and handed me his opera glasses, not for play but for a specific purpose: so that I could see. Of course, anyone who knew him, or knew about him, or argued a case in front of him knew that he treasured clarity. He loved to kibitz (as he put it) about law, history, philosophy, and religion in order to clarify things. He loved the intricacies of grammar and vocabulary because those are necessary for expressing thought clearly. This desire for clarity extended to the faith as well.

My parents grew up in a seeming golden age of the Catholic Church in the United States. In the 1940s and '50s, Catholics had come into their own in every part of society, while retaining (for the most part) a good sense about what it meant to be Catholic. Mom and Dad married in 1960, and over the next ten years, it seemed as though the bottom had fallen out of the Church. Priests and nuns abandoned their vocations at a dizzying rate. The Mass was abruptly changed—and then those changes were abused. My mother recalls that when *Humanae vitae* was released, the priest told the congregation not to worry, that he and other priests were going to meet with the bishop "to see what can be done about it".

Through these confused and confusing years, Dad sought to provide clarity. Wherever we lived, he and Mom always found a parish that provided faithful teaching and a reverent Mass. One of my earliest memories is looking up at the mosaics in St. Matthew Cathedral in Washington, D.C.—where Dad's desire for clarity had brought us from suburban Virginia on Sundays. When we lived in Chicago, Dad drove us a half hour each way every Sunday to a parish where he was confident the faith would be clearly presented.

"Listen, my son" is a phrase we encounter often in Scripture's wisdom literature. It captures the voice of a father seeking to enlighten his son, so that the son can see the way and walk in it. It is a proper fatherly task. A man fathers children not just by a physical act but also by providing that clarity and purpose essential for life. "Where there is no vision, the people perish" (Prov 29:18, KJV).

Finally, my father gave me a sense of transcendence. Dad put me on his shoulders so that I could see beyond him, to another father, the pope. In itself, it was not a particularly transcendent experience. But in light of it, I recall those other moments when Dad—by word and action— pointed us beyond himself. The memory of him and Mom kneeling in the sand at an otherwise irreverent Mass at the beach; of his loading us up in the car to go pray at the church for a dying friend of his; of his concentration in prayer after receiving Holy Communion. I take more than a little delight in remembering when a visiting priest got the better of him in an argument about faith—and brought him to a reverent and humble silence.

"Call no man your father" (Mt 23:9). This striking command of Our Lord reminds us that, as the ancient saying has it, *nemo tam patris*—no one is father as God is Father. Being a father means not just yielding to this transcendent Fatherhood but also pointing beyond oneself to the One from Whom all fatherhood on earth is named (see Eph 3:14–15).

Finally, and perhaps most importantly, I remember it all as so ordinary and natural. Identity, clarity, transcendence—these did not enter my father's mind as he hoisted me onto his shoulders. He was not thinking about fatherhood, much less about its transcendent purposes. And if he had been, something about that moment would have been lost. No, he was simply being a father, doing what a dad naturally does for his child. But when a father does that—simply, naturally, plainly—God gives the grace for it to become something much more.

8

# Mary Shivanandan

*Since the 1970s Mary Shivanandan has researched and written articles from a Catholic perspective on marriage and family. In 1988 she was awarded a fellowship to the John Paul II Institute for Studies on Marriage and Family, where she both taught and completed the STL and STD degrees. Her most notable books are* Natural Sex, *of which portions were later reissued as* Challenge to Love, *and* Crossing the Threshold of Love: A New Vision of Marriage in the Light of John Paul II's Anthropology, *published in 1999 and reprinted by Bloomsbury International in 2014. Her book* The Holy Family: Model, Not Exception *is the fruit of her teaching at the Institute. Dr. Shivanandan is a mother and a grandmother. For a more detailed biography, visit www.MaryShivanandan.com.*

In November 1979, the United Kingdom publisher of my book *Natural Sex* sent me on a publicity tour of Dublin, Belfast, and London. Barricades and security checks marked our visit to Belfast. The hotel we stayed in had been blown up and rebuilt six times. British soldiers with bayonets at the ready surprised us around a street corner as we walked to the radio station.

A reporter from a Belfast newspaper who interviewed me was far more interested in my Protestant-Catholic background than in the subject matter of my book. She had joined the women's peace movement in Northern

Ireland and was saddened to see that bright hope of recon-
ciliation shattered by the hatred of centuries at that time.

Each of us has our personal family dramas. My own
family solved its religious differences more pragmatically
than consciously. We were brought up as Catholics, but all
contact with our Irish relatives was cut off. This creates in
a child a kind of schizophrenia, which results, it seems to
me, in either a deeper suppression of the forbidden identity or a search for wholeness.

I personally longed for that wholeness but was also
afraid of it. The trip to Dublin presented the opportunity
to restore ties to a lost family. I was not looking for it. A
cousin who chanced to read a newspaper article on me
and my book telephoned me in London. For the first time,
I learned that I had cousins in the United States. All my
father's brothers and sisters had died. Only the youngest
sister survived and lived a mere two hundred miles from
our home in Washington, D.C.

What kind of emotions accompanies the discovery of
such a close family tie after nearly half a century of silence?
For me, it was too deep for words, but I experienced
an unlocking of forbidden areas, a shattering of myths
and prejudices; I had been brought up without a sense
of belonging.

I was surprised that the Irish side of the family knew
more about us than we knew about them. They had never
stopped caring about us. We were still a part of the family
but one that had strayed out of focus. That unequivocal
acceptance was a healing experience. My father was not
just a father but a brother, a son, and a grandson. For the
first time, I saw photos of my grandparents, uncles, aunts,
and cousins. I could pick out family resemblances. My
aunt gave me mementoes of my father: a decorated Bur-
mese dagger, an embossed cigarette case, a golfing trophy.

These I can pass on to my children—tangible and intangible keys to their identity.

But I need to go back even further to explain how my father passed on the Catholic faith and how, in spite of my being able to spend only two years in his presence, that faith has been his great gift to me.

As the eldest son of a large, devout, Irish Catholic family, my father had been encouraged to enter the seminary, so he was enrolled in Maynooth, the premier seminary in Ireland. After four years at the seminary, he determined that he did not have a vocation to the priesthood. He had the opportunity to sit for the civil service exams in England that recruited bright young men for government service either at home or in the "empire". We have one of the few photos of him as a dashing young man about town in a bowler hat and spats. (A photo toward the end of his career shows him seated in black tie and tails, with the Star of India medal at his throat, a row of medals on his chest, and a sword in its scabbard at his side—ready for dinner at the viceroy of India's palace.)

My father passed the exams and opted for service in Burma, because, my mother later said, it had the largest allowances. Indeed, compared with India, Burma, which at that time was administered as part of India by the Indian Civil Service, was considered a hardship post because of its climate and the frequency of disease. As an avid golfer, my father along with another up-country district officer carved a nine-hole golf course out of the jungle. I know little else about his life at that time because by the time he met my mother, he was posted in Rangoon, the capital. As many others did, he sought a wife while on leave in England. I understand the last time he visited Ireland was in 1924, possibly because of the rising Irish independence movement. At any rate, he proposed to and was accepted by my mother, who came from a staunch but nonpracticing Scots Presbyterian family.

Although my father was not practicing his faith either, he opted for a Catholic wedding at St. John's Catholic Church in Rangoon. Later my husband and I, on a visit to Rangoon, were able to secure a copy of their wedding certificate and my baptismal certificate, which had survived Japanese occupation during the Second World War. These early years turned out to be the most time I spent with my father. Because of the threat of disease—a friend had lost her three young sons to disease—it was decided that my four-year-old sister, my three-year-old brother, and I, age eighteen months, would be sent to a boarding school in England for children whose parents were abroad. The usual age at which children were sent home from India for education was seven. The deleterious effects that such institutional care would have on very young children were not known at the time. This is not to say we had no family life after that time. When I was six, we sailed to India for a three-month stay in New Delhi, which I remember as a very happy time, since we were all together as a family. It was at the school in England the next year that I received my First Communion.

The move to England, however, was only the first uprooting. Enter World War II and the very real threat of an invasion of England. Once more, our parents were challenged to secure safety for us. As I remember, often by twos and threes, the children at the school would disappear, some to Canada, others to the United States or South Africa. Then it was our turn to leave. With three hundred other children, we were put on a liner destined for Australia. With my father's posting in New Delhi, Sydney was much closer than Canada would have been. But that was before the Japanese entered the war and cut all travel between India and Australia.

We were sent to the very best Catholic schools in Sydney at considerable sacrifice. Only later did I learn from Irish relatives that my father, at the same time, was supporting two nephews' seminary education in Maynooth. The education we received at these schools, especially in religion at that time, was solidly grounded in the faith. My father had been a brilliant classicist. From his encouragement I had acquired a love of learning (I later read classics at Cambridge University). From my education at school and from my father, I never doubted the intellectual foundations of the faith. The philosophy of Plato and Aristotle, especially the latter's treatises on natural law, proved a providential preparation for my later work on the Church's teaching in Pope Paul VI's encyclical *Humanae vitae*. It was also a fitting introduction to the theology of Saints Thomas Aquinas and John Paul II at the John Paul II Institute for Studies on Marriage and Family at the Catholic University of America.

What was more of a challenge, given my lack of family life, was the reality of God as love. It may seem strange, but the lay sisters at the school proved to be my inspiration. I would watch them outside in the courtyard in the depths of winter, peeling potatoes for our meal. When they came to Communion after the choir nuns, their habits reeked from their kitchen duties. I intuitively knew that only a great love could induce them to live such a hard, hidden life. Another great gift was Mary, given as Mother to every baptized Christian. In my eyes, I had three mothers: one perfect, our mother in Heaven, and two imperfect, my absent mother who gave me life and the mistress general of the school who was our guardian. As a nun in a position of authority, she could not show special love to one child in the school, but I knew she loved me. Of course, the nanny, who nursed me from birth to eighteen months, was also important. As she was paid, her care could not be unconditional, so she could only abandon us to the institution.

It took many years to recover from the deprivations of childhood. Not only were we virtually brought up as orphans or foster children—generous families in Australia would take us in for the holidays—but when I was seventeen, my father was shot and killed by armed robbers. A year later, I was diagnosed with tuberculosis, which entailed nine months in the hospital and a sanitarium. I doubt I would have survived without the gift of faith given me by my father. Much healing has come through the daily Eucharist, in addition to two years of visits to a Catholic psychiatrist before marriage.

Since prejudice against Catholics—not open, aggressive prejudice but subtle racial prejudice—existed in England in the 1950s, I learned to hide my religious affiliation until I had first established ties on a human level. When such ties had been thoroughly established, I would casually reveal my Catholicism. The response was often "But you're quite normal, not peculiar at all." My father's commitment to our Catholic education, even though he did not practice, had a profound effect on strengthening my commitment to the faith. That has been invaluable in navigating a world that is increasingly secularist and hostile to Christianity.

I never had the time to discuss with my father the morality of colonialism, but I distinctly remember his saying that he would have voted for Clement Atlee, the Labor leader, who planned to give up any vestiges of colonialism. My father was also invited to continue contributing his expertise to the independent government of Pakistan. He declined because he still had to finance our university education and so took a position with the British Control

Commission in Germany, where he met his death. Incidentally, my sister told me that two weeks before his death, he had seen a priest, a gift of grace, since he could not have known his life would end so soon.

My father's gift of faith did not end there. It was instrumental in my finally overcoming my prejudices and marrying my Sri Lankan husband, a marriage that lasted all but fifty years. When it was clear, after two years of courtship, that he wanted to marry me, I remonstrated that, first, he was not Catholic and, second, I had been brought up in a somewhat prejudiced environment. He responded that if I could admit it, I could get over it. Also, he believed that prejudice was more about our relationship with God than with man. Indeed, I recall from my childhood a picture that had a powerful effect on me: of Christ opening His arms to children of all races. As my husband had already been exposed to the Christian faith, he converted and developed a deep devotion to the Rosary and to the Sacred Heart of Jesus.

Originally we settled on a house in northern Virginia, but because the anti-miscegenation laws were still on the books in Virginia, we bought a house in Maryland. When Martin Luther King was assassinated, we were celebrating my daughter's fourth birthday with Sri Lankan, Caucasian, and African American guests. Not only did my husband faithfully attend Sunday Mass at our local parish, but he went out of his way to be friends with our neighbors, one of whom said that watching us as he grew up gave him the courage to marry an African American.

These might not seem to the casual observer to be direct gifts from my father's faith, but I am certain that they flowed from his subtle, yet powerful, love of the Church, for which I am forever grateful.

# 9

# Jim Burnham

*Jim Burnham is a Catholic evangelist and apologist. He is the coauthor of the immensely popular series Beginning Apologetics. These short, easy-to-read handbooks equip Catholics to answer charitably the most common questions about and objections to their Catholic faith. With Steve Wood, editor of Dads.org, Jim is also the coauthor of* Christian Fatherhood *(Family Life Center, 1997)—wherein this essay originally appeared—a manual for raising Catholic children in the modern world. All these resources are available at CatholicApologetics.com and Catholic bookstores everywhere. Jim gives exciting apologetics conferences all over the country. He lives in Pasadena, California, with his wife, Lisa, and their six children.*

If I have any weaknesses as a father, I have only myself to blame. In this age of victims, dysfunctional families, and easy alibis, I simply have no excuse. God blessed me with wonderful role models in my father and mother. Their lives are an enduring testimony of faithfulness to God and family. So, if I have any strengths as a father, it is only because I stand on the shoulders of giants.

We buried my father, David Burnham, thirteen months ago [in November 1993]. Just why God allowed him to die at the age of fifty-three, when six of his ten children still lived at home, the youngest only eleven years old, is a mystery to me. Sometimes I am tempted to shake my fist at God and ask in Job-like indignation, "Why, Lord? Why would You, a loving Father, take my loving father from the family that needs him so desperately?" But in the midst of my grief and in those moments of not-so-quiet desperation, I find some consolation and strength in the heritage my father left behind.

Admittedly, that consolation can be very small. What I want is his larger-than-life presence and his seemingly inexhaustible wisdom. I want him to tell me how to handle my two-year-old's tantrums and how to protect my children from the seductions of our age. What I have is a handful of memories and the poor copy of his legacy that I reflect in my character. But these deposits still hold his examples and convictions and, with God's grace, will guide my own fathering.

David Burnham was a man of surpassing faithfulness to his Church, his family, and his principles. As a husband and father, he understood that he was the domestic priest who had a fundamental obligation to help every member of his family become a saint.

As priest of the home, Dad exercised a vigilant watch over our spiritual development. He insisted that we receive the sacraments frequently and that we learn to love and live our faith. Every morning on the way to Mass, he would give us a mini sermon on the essential doctrines of our faith. Sometimes after dinner, he would read from the Bible or a favorite spiritual book.

Dad loved and respected the Catholic Church. He would tolerate no criticism of priests, pointing out that only they can bring Our Lord to us in the Holy Eucharist. Whenever possible, he took the whole family to daily Mass, and he often told us, "Any career that doesn't allow time for daily Mass isn't much of a career." He stressed that just "going through the motions" of prayer, Mass, and other sacraments was no guarantee of sanctity. "Rubbing shoulders with Christ won't help unless He rubs off on you," he would say, "for Judas spent three years with Christ, and yet Judas was probably lost."

My father put his family second only to God. Early in his marriage, Dad set a goal to have a business that would support him without consuming him. For the last twelve years of his life, he ran a successful real estate company from his office at home, amid constant interruptions from the younger children, who were being homeschooled. Never too busy to give advice, never too tired to discipline, he poured out his life in service to his family.

Dad often told us that he loved us, and he *always* did so after he disciplined us. He spanked for only two offenses: disobedience and a bad attitude. Being both willful and temperamental, I was notorious for receiving the lion's share of spankings! But I received a lion's share of affirmation as well.

Dad taught us to communicate honestly and to apologize promptly. He was always willing to listen—even in an argument—and if he was wrong, he quickly and sincerely asked for our forgiveness.

My father was generous with his time, money, and wisdom. He made time to counsel family and friends. He tithed to acknowledge the Lordship of Christ over his finances, and he encouraged his children to do the same. He taught us to work when we were very young, to save money, and to be responsible for our luxuries. In first grade, when I told my dad I wanted a new bike, he took me to the *Daily Times* and showed me how to peddle newspapers to the local businesses after school.

My father was a chaste man in a sex-soaked society. He was pure in speech and in mind. I never knew him to tell an off-color joke or look lustfully at a woman. He taught his children modesty and chastity through the fidelity and respect he showed my mother, Peggy, his wife of twenty-seven years.

Dad was thrilled to be alive. "Every day above ground is a good day", he'd quote from some otherwise forgettable movie. He loved being out in God's creation: farming, fishing, flying, trail riding, scuba diving, and subdividing. He taught us that God's creation can be enjoyed fully if it is used in His service.

My father was full of joy. His greatest charm was that he truly loved people. He made friends everywhere because of his winning smile and genuine emotion. He had a joke or a story or a saying for every occasion; some of his favorites he told again and again until they became family proverbs: "I'd give my right arm to be ambidextrous" or "He's busier than a one-legged man in a dance contest."

My father was the most courageous man I ever knew. Friends and enemies alike regarded him as a man of integrity. Dad had the courage of his convictions. He fought tirelessly for the causes he knew were right, no matter what the consequences. As a member of the local school board, he was often outvoted four to one as he fought against sex education and funding for faculty abortions. On the feast of the Holy Innocents, he took his family to stand in front of the Planned Parenthood clinic to protest the slaughter of unborn children. For many years, he gave pro-life classes to the seniors at the local public high school. Shortly before he died, he erected a billboard that still declares to twenty-five thousand passing cars every day: "Adoption, Not Abortion".

Even during his battle with cancer, Dad's faith never faltered. While he hated the thought of dying, he did not grow angry with God. He fought death with every ounce of his strength, but his battle cry was: "If God wants me to go, nothing can keep me; if God wants me to stay, nothing can take me." Dad told us on the Tuesday before he died that it was his Holy Week, that he was going "home", and that we should pray for the strength to go on after he was gone. It reminded me of Christ's words to the weeping women of Jerusalem, consoling them in the midst of His own terrible agony. While we children still lived at home, Dad would bless and kiss each of us good night. As we got older, this simple ritual became an increasingly precious way of saying "I love you." Before I left Dad that last day at the hospital, I leaned over his bed to kiss him goodbye. He weakly raised his hand and blessed me for the last time. I couldn't stop the tears—he was a father and a family priest to the very end.

We brought him home the afternoon before he died. He had received all his sacraments and the apostolic blessing. That night, we gathered around him and read his favorite poems. Dad died peacefully as we read from the psalms of his namesake, King David. Although the cancer ravaged his body, it purified his soul and confirmed his faith. As his strength failed, his eyes grew ever more luminous. Dad had often said, "The only mistake you can make in life is not to die a saint." Considering the way he lived and the way he died, I trust, by the grace and mercy of God, that he did not make that mistake.

When I wallow in self-pity, asking why I had only twenty-six years with my father, I have to stop and remember that at least I had twenty-six wonderful years with my dad. My younger brothers and sisters received much less. I know that many children don't have good role models; many children grow up without fathers at all. How can this tribute to my father apply to them?

After all, I'm a cradle-Catholic father who was given every ingredient to become a good father. What about those fathers who didn't even have a recipe? To answer this heartfelt concern, I should mention that David Burnham's own father—an upright man—was a nonpracticing Mormon who often worked away from home from the time my dad was six. He died when Dad was only twelve.

Although he didn't have many years with his dad, my father managed to leave an enduring legacy for his children. He made up, in one generation, all that had been lacking in his own upbringing. I am capable of undoing, in one generation, all that has been entrusted to me. One generation is all it takes; one generation is all we have.

As fathers, we have an obligation to give even more than we have received. Let us father our families in such a way that when we die, our children will be able to stand on our shoulders and say: "I had such a wonderful father that if I have any weaknesses as a parent, I have only myself to blame."

# 10

# Father Jerome T. Karcher

*Father Jerome Karcher was born and raised in Anaheim, California, the seventh of twelve children of Carl and Margaret Karcher. His father is the founder of the popular fast-food chain Carl's Jr. Having attended the University of San Diego and Gonzaga University in Florence, Italy, Father Karcher graduated from Loyola University of Los Angeles with a bachelor of arts degree in psychology. He entered the Dominican Order and received a degree in philosophy from the Dominican School of Philosophy and Theology at the Graduate Theological Union in Berkeley, California, where he also studied theology. He completed his theological studies and earned a master of arts degree at Saint John's Seminary in Camarillo, California. On February 12, 1983, Father Karcher was ordained to the priesthood by Bishop William Johnson for the service of the Roman Catholic Diocese of Orange in California. He is the pastor of Saint Vincent de Paul Church in Huntington Beach, California (www.svdphb.org), where he promotes evangelization using the Alpha Course with a desire to draw people into a deeper relationship with Jesus in the Church and a life in the sacraments, especially the Eucharist. Father Karcher is the founder and chairman of the board of Mercy House Living Centers (www.mercyhouse.net), which provides housing and comprehensive supportive services for a variety of homeless populations, including families, adult men and women, mothers and their children, persons living with HIV or AIDS, individuals overcoming substance addictions, and persons who are physically and mentally disabled.*

I remember standing in the kitchen at home with my parents one evening, having just returned from Saint Albert's Priory—the Dominican House of Studies in Oakland—where I had spent Holy Week as an observer interested in religious life. My siblings had wondered where I went during the Easter break, but my parents were sworn to secrecy—just telling them that I was traveling! I wanted to wait to tell them about my interest in a vocation to the priesthood until I had more certainty. That spring evening, I told my parents that I was going to apply for admission to the Dominican novitiate. My father told me that it would be a great blessing for the family if I were to be ordained a priest. But he added that if, for whatever reason, I decided that it was not my vocation, I would always be welcomed home. These words from my father and his openness to God's plan for me, however it worked out, were a sign of his deep faith. Allow me to share parts of his life with you.

My father, Carl Nicholas Karcher, was the very definition of a man of the people. It might be better to say that he was a man *for* the people. Once you met him, you would always remember him, and he would remember you. He would greet you with his strong voice, his hearty, sincere handshake, and his expansive countenance, which seemed to enclose you with him in a private conversation.

"How are you?" was his calling card. He always looked right at you, never intimidating but emitting a warmth that seemed to come from some inner reservoir of goodwill. It bespoke his true character: "How are you?" is what he said, for meeting my dad was not so much about him as it was about you. And you remembered.

He had a remarkable memory for recalling names and the uncanny ability to recite the exact date of a previous encounter with almost anyone he had met. When you met him, the founder of Carl's Jr. Restaurants, you would walk away with a personally signed card entitling you to a free Carl's Jr. Famous Star Hamburger. That card was placed inside a prayer card that expressed his gratitude and spirituality with his favorite family prayer: the Prayer of Saint Francis of Assisi. He never left home without a small stack of these cards, which he loved to pass out. Often, people kept them as a memento of their meeting and never redeemed them for a meal.

For many, the experience of meeting Carl Karcher occurred at a community event, perhaps at a business lunch or a charity function. Throughout the years, he was frequently seen at notable Orange County and Southern California social occasions, especially those dedicated to charities. Certainly, the man the public saw and encountered was part of who he was. But the true measure of this man is what he did for others quietly, away from the public eye. In this light, my father was a man of deep convictions with an unwavering Catholic faith anchored in his family life.

Friends, relatives, and guests who visited the Karcher household were readily absorbed into the family mix. Dad was outgoing, smart, and quick-witted and had a great sense of humor. He enjoyed conversations, telling stories, and hamming it up with plenty of jokes and pranks. He played a mean game of ping-pong and loved fast-paced games—the quicker, the better. Part of his Ohio legacy was a card game known as Cassini, which he played with all of his children and grandchildren for hours at family gatherings.

My dad was born on January 16, 1917, in the pure farm country of northern Ohio, the heartland of America. The roots of his Midwestern upbringing were always in his soul. From his birthplace he absorbed the deep, traditional values of the American hearthstone: honesty in dealing with others, perseverance, and hard work within a stable framework of the nuclear family. And he was a man of faith—a deep, abiding, penetrating faith in God, Who directed and guided him through the teachings of Jesus Christ in the Catholic Church. This faith was, for him, always his bedrock, his core.

As a young adult, my father made several trips to California. When he finally came to California to stay, it was for a young lady whom he would love with all his heart for the rest of his life, Margaret Magdalen Heinz. It was in her that the values of his young life were to be realized. With my mother he raised twelve children, and he immersed himself in their upbringing. His family was his life.

Throughout his married life, my father would most often introduce my mother as "my bride" rather than "my wife", which always provided a certain freshness to their marriage. He deeply respected this most important woman in his life, his beloved wife of sixty-six years, whom he lost to cancer in June 2006 and missed every day of his remaining life. Margaret was his partner and companion not only in family life but in business as well. She operated his first hotdog carts when my dad was in the service during World War II; and she served on the board of directors when Carl Karcher Enterprises became a world-class corporation. She was a stay-at-home mom and the center of support for my father.

At the heart of my father's life was his Catholic faith. If you wanted to see Carl on any given day, you had to rise early. You would find him at Saint Boniface Catholic Church in Anaheim attending Mass every day, usually at 6:30 in the morning, preceded by quiet time praying his novenas and devotions at home. That was usually after two hours of personal work at home in the wee morning hours. He would go to the office only after time in prayer in the church and receiving the Holy Eucharist, the true sustenance for his active life.

Saint Boniface was the parish church where he and my mother were married and brought us every Sunday for Mass. It was there that their sons and daughters were raised in the faith and where his family celebrated Baptisms, First Communions, Confirmations, weddings, funerals, a first priestly Mass, and many other liturgical benchmarks.

At the end of the day, Dad returned home—never missing family dinner—to the house in Anaheim that he and my mother had purchased in 1949 when they had five children. Seven more would be raised in that same home. Each night after dinner, the entire family would spend half an hour praying the Rosary around the dinner table. This influenced my devotion to the Rosary and my confidence in the Blessed Mother's maternal intercession in my life and my priesthood. During Lent, Dad and Mom would bring all twelve children to Mass each morning. On First Fridays and First Saturdays, my parents and the older children would pray the Rosary, kneeling before the statues of the Sacred Heart of Jesus and the Immaculate Heart of Mary. These times of prayer were the true center of our family life, obtaining divine protection and graces, which we would quietly and inwardly receive.

In the last few years of his life, living with Parkinson's disease, my dad experienced a diminished ability to speak clearly. This made him a bit quieter in the public eye. At home, however, he continued to be a communicator, even when he could not get the words out easily. Every grandchild knew that three knocks on the table meant "I love you", and then Dad would wrap his large hands around the little hands of each grandchild to complete the message. Such expressions of affection in the face of a crippling disease ennobled his life and were an inspiration to all of us in his family. Even when it became difficult for him to enunciate, he would manage a recognizable "thank you, son" or "thank you, dear" to whoever helped him stand up or walked with him up the stairs. True to his nature, he was resolute in his efforts to climb the long staircase in his home until the very end.

Even with Parkinson's, he insisted on kneeling during the Consecration at Mass, knowing that he was in the presence of Jesus. This humility before God was a great grace in his life.

My father passed away on a Friday evening, January 11, 2008, five days before his ninety-first birthday, surrounded prayerfully by his children and grandchildren. It was a grace to pray with my dad until the end, seeing him receive the sacraments. His obituary paid tribute to his full life as recounted here and remembered among my dad's eleven living children: Anne Wiles, Patricia LaGraffe, Margaret LeVecke, Carl Leo Karcher, Kadie Karcher, Father Jerome Karcher, Janelle Karcher, Rosemary Miller, Barbara Wall, Joseph Karcher, and Mary Miller. My sister Carleen Karcher had died in April 1993.

Dad's nearly ninety-one years spanned an era from the horse and buggy at his farm in Ohio to space travel; from a single hot-dog cart to an international fast-food corporation; from Ohio farm boy to father of a family of twelve children, fifty-one grandchildren, and forty-five great-grandchildren. He remained gracious, generous, and grateful until the day he passed on.

In some ways, my father was larger than life. He was an icon that so many people respected—a man who faithfully lived his commitments to God, his family, his co-workers at Carl Karcher Enterprises, and his country. His gregarious personality, his large stature, his accessible and friendly manner, his Horatio Alger–type success story, his Catholic beliefs and generous smile were all very engaging and sincere. All of these made him a great man.

But truly great men are great because they see something, Someone, greater than themselves. Even in their greatness, they know that they rely on God for everything. They know that this world is passing; and they anchor their hope in something more than this world. And this "more" is God Himself. Saint Paul reminds us that we look "not to the things that are seen but to the things that are unseen; for the things that are seen are transient, but the things that are unseen are eternal" (2 Cor 4:18).

My father's love was generous—as generous as his unforgettable handshake: large, embracing, and full. It was bigger than life. His large farm-boy hands milked cows and hauled hay in from the plowed fields in Ohio. Those same hands generously passed out hamburger coupons and prayer cards to everyone. But once inside the church, those hands blessed him with holy water as he folded them in prayer.

My dad's greatest and most important legacy is his Catholic faith and devotion to the Holy Eucharist. His love for the Eucharist drew me as a young man to attend daily Mass (Dad would attend in the early morning and I in the evening). At Mass, the words of Jesus would always be a strengthening balm for my dad. He would hear the words of Jesus: "This is my Body. This is my Blood." He would receive Holy Communion to be strengthened by the very presence of God, Who transforms simple bread and wine into the Body and Blood of Jesus Christ. Nothing was more important to him than participating in the Mass, during which the saving sacrifice and Resurrection of Jesus is made present; sharing this holy meal, this promise of the eternal banquet in Heaven, knowing that there is a world beyond that God has prepared for us. Saint Paul reminds us that even as our outer self is wasting away, we are not discouraged because our inner self is being renewed day by day (2 Cor 4:16).

The night my father died, I called a priest friend and told him that Dad had passed away. The friend replied, "Finally, he will see Margaret again." I paused for a moment and said: "Maybe he will even bump into Jesus there!" That is the point!

In a very human way, people yearn to see those loved ones who have gone before them. Indeed, this will be one of the great gifts of heavenly life. But first there will be a meeting with Jesus, Who, I imagine, would take my father by the hand and present him to God the Father, bringing him to that heavenly throne where he would see Almighty God face-to-face. And there my dad would be with Mary, our Blessed Mother, who had interceded for him; there she would remember the many times my dad would have prayed, "Holy Mary, Mother of God, pray for us sinners now and at the hour of our death." And, in fact, she would remember and be there to escort my father to his bride of many years, my mother standing nearby, radiant with joy at the final homecoming, when my dad, purified by God's grace—washed clean—would join that great cloud of witnesses in the Body of Christ, giving praise and thanks to God for His generous and everlasting mercy and love. My dad would encounter the same Jesus he encountered every day in the Eucharist, in Holy Communion, which unites people with the entire Body of Christ and all of the members of the Church from the beginning to the end of time.

Our longing for Heaven is a grace that my father modeled for me and my family. His disciplined witness to the faith, his deep convictions, and his great work ethic inspired us and challenged us. As his son, I have benefited from his generosity of spirit and his life of prayer. He was always

supportive of me in my vocation to the priesthood—
always supportive but never demanding. From my father,
I always sensed that our daily family Rosary brought a
residual grace—a lasting grace—that would be accessed
along the way of our lives, even unknowingly. At the end,
my dad would experience that greatest healing, that greatest gift, the gift of salvation in Jesus Christ.

# Abby Johnson

*As one of the youngest Planned Parenthood clinic directors in the nation, Abby Johnson believed in a woman's right to choose—until the day she saw something that changed everything. After participating in an ultrasound-guided abortion, Abby left Planned Parenthood and joined the pro-life movement. She is the author of two best-selling books,* Unplanned *and* The Walls Are Talking. *Her book* Unplanned *has been turned into a major motion picture and was released in spring 2019. Abby is the founder and CEO of And Then There Were None and Pro-Love Ministries. She lives in Texas with her husband and eight children. Her family came into the Catholic Church in 2012.*

I remember standing at the top of the stairs, looking down at the water below me. The pastor had told me it would be warm, but I was still nervous to get in. Even as an eight-year-old child, I knew that walking into that water meant something special. I had prayed the Sinner's Prayer and had given my heart to Jesus. I wasn't exactly sure what that meant, but I knew I didn't want to go to Hell, and I knew that I really did love Jesus. The pastor had told me that if I really wanted Jesus to be in my heart, then the next step after the prayer was Baptism. I really did want Jesus to live in my heart.

I stepped in and surprisingly, the water was very warm. It felt as if I were stepping into a bathtub. My pastor was already in, helping me get situated in the water. It felt weird to be in the water with all those clothes on. The pastor asked me if I had accepted Jesus into my heart. I said that I had. He asked me if I was ready to be baptized and make it public that I was a Christian. I said yes to that too. "Then I baptize you, Abby, in the name of the Father, Son, and Holy Spirit." I held my nose and fell backward into the water. As I came up, I wiped my eyes and saw my dad standing at the top of the stairs. He was beaming, smiling from ear to ear. Everyone in the congregation clapped, and I climbed up the stairs. I gave my dad a hug and realized that now it was his turn.

I watched him go into the water and come up, and I felt such relief. "Whew, now Dad and I will be in Heaven together," I thought. I didn't really understand that my dad was already a Christian. He had simply never been baptized by full submersion, and that is required in the Baptist faith. A sprinkle as a baby won't cut it for the Baptist church. My dad had been raised Methodist, and by joining the Baptist church, he had to be fully submerged. So we decided to do it together, Easter 1989. And that's my dad. He has always been beside me at the important times of my life—his faith an example of the faith that I would one day strive to have.

That's the example my father has always been for me and my mom. He has been the epitome of provider, protector, father, and husband. He showed me how a husband should love his wife. He showed me how a father should love his children.

My dad has spent his career as a mechanical engineer. He's not only wise but also very intelligent. I grew up believing that I could do anything I put my mind to. Education was vitally important in our home. My dad wanted me to research on my own, make decisions on my own, and find my own path. I'm sure he and my mom never guessed that path would lead me to the doors of Planned Parenthood.

Looking back, I can't even imagine how hard my eight years there must have been for my parents. They had to strike a delicate balance: always being proud of me and, at the same time, hating my work. This strong work ethic that I received from my father must have felt like a double-edged sword at times for him. Yes, he wanted me to believe I could be anything, but never, ever thought I would want to be an abortion facility director.

My dad has always had a very strong faith but is pretty reserved. My mom is the one who wears everything on her sleeve. After I had worked in the abortion facility for eight years, my mom had become exasperated. One night, after a phone call with me, she let her frustration out. She said to my dad, "She is just never going to get out of there. I don't understand how she doesn't see what she's doing." I wasn't there for the conversation, but I imagine that, after hearing my mom's outburst, my dad slowly looked up from the paper, took his reading glasses off, and set them on the table beside him before replying, "God has promised us that she will return to Him. Scripture tells us that as long as we raise our children knowing the Lord, then they will always return. We may not be here to see it, but we have to trust that it will happen."

Just one month later, I called my parents to tell them that I had just left the clinic for the last time. They were on vacation, but I didn't want to wait to tell them. I called and asked what they were doing. "Driving around Estes Park," my mom said. I asked her to put the speaker on so that Dad could hear me while I gave the big news.

"I quit my job at Planned Parenthood," I said.

It was quiet for just a few seconds before I heard my mom exclaim, "Are you serious? You quit!" Then all I could hear was laughing and crying and what could only be described as joyful noises in their car. It suddenly got quiet again, and my dad spoke up. "Abby, do you need us to send you money?" That was my dad, the perpetual provider. Even through all the excitement, it was as if my dad sensed what could be coming. Leaving my job, my friends, my steady income—it would come with a cost. And while I knew he had to be beaming with pride that his prayers had been answered, he never stopped worrying. He never stopped being Dad.

I'm proud that my dad has been able to see me grow into the woman he wanted me to be. I'm proud that he can see that the strong work ethic he instilled in me is now being used to proclaim life. No matter where I have been in life—being baptized as a child, graduating from high school and then college, working at Planned Parenthood, having my children, sitting at the premiere of my film—he has always been there to support me. He has loved me so well throughout my life, and I pray that the faith that I have watched him live out will be abundantly evident in the faith that I share with my children.

# 12

# Frank J. Hanna

*Frank J. Hanna lives in Atlanta, Georgia. He invests as a mer-*
*chant banker in technology and financial services and has started*
*and sold numerous businesses over the last three decades. He has*
*been involved in education for thirty-eight years and has been*
*instrumental in the foundation of thirteen educational institutions,*
*from preschool through postsecondary. He is a frequent speaker to*
*various groups and to the mass media regarding macroeconomics,*
*education, and philanthropy, authoring two best-selling books,*
What Your Money Means *and* A Graduate's Guide to
Life. *He serves on and advises the boards of numerous Catholic*
*and other nonprofit organizations, including EWTN, the Acton*
*Institute, and the American Enterprise Institute. Frank founded*
*the Solidarity Association, which donated to the Vatican Apos-*
*tolic Library the oldest copy of the Lord's Prayer in the world. He*
*was named a Knight Grand Cross of the Order of Saint Gregory*
*by Pope Benedict XVI.*

My father is an unconventional man, and most folks sense
this almost immediately when they meet him. His forth-
rightness, his surprising comments, the sense that you are
not sure what he is going to do next—all of this together
tends to throw people off their balance for just a moment.
It is slightly discombobulating for them, but they seem to
like it—sort of like the first jolt when the roller coaster
starts. There is a feeling of "Well, here we go!"

I share my father's name. As an adult, whenever I would meet someone who knew my father, I inevitably knew what that person would say to me. First, the question "Is Frank Hanna your dad?" And when I would answer yes, almost like clockwork, the next thing the person said would be "I gotta tell you, I love your dad!"

My father is smart, engaging, creative, industrious, and disciplined, but also a bit crazy and unpredictable. So I have asked myself, "Why is it that people always feel the need to tell me that they love my dad? And why do I love him so much?" I mean, I know he has his good qualities, but I also know his faults, and the feelings of affection that he engenders in others seem almost disproportionate. And as I reflected further on the matter, I realized that my dad has three attributes that, when combined, create an overwhelming positive impression on people:

- He is steadfastly loyal.
- He is unashamed to tell you he loves you and cares for you.
- He is unabashedly sincere and enthusiastic in encouraging the well-being of others, in a way completely divorced from the normal envy and jealousy we meet in the world, even from relatives and friends. This trait is so striking that it can be incredibly inspirational. You leave an encounter with him feeling filled with the Spirit.

It was through the example of these three qualities—loyalty, affection, and encouragement—that my father taught me about God.

When I was a little boy, and even today at fifty-eight years old, and for all the time in between, my father never passed up an opportunity to give me a hug and to tell

me he loved me. As a little boy, I knew the feel of the
five-o'clock shadow on his face in the evening, for when
my siblings and I would greet him after work, we would
always receive a hug and a kiss. We received another one
when he would tuck us in at night. My brother and I slept
in the same room. Each night he would give us a hug, kiss
us, and say, "Good night, Superboy. I love you", and each
of us would respond, "Love you too, Superdad."

We were blessed, because we did not go through
life wondering whether our father loved us. We knew.
We knew, not only because he told us sometimes but
because he told us *every night*! And not only because he
told us, but because *he was there* every night to tell us. A
lot of life is all about showing up, and boy, did my dad
show up! He always showed up. He was always there. He
always had our backs. When I was a child, my father was
very busy. He had a full-time job and worked on the side
building another business. But my brother, my sister, and
I never had any question about whether he had time for
us—we came first, before anything.

I don't recall my father's being all that explicit in teaching us about our faith. We always said a blessing at dinner,
but other than that, we did not usually pray together at
home as a family. Notably, though, we never missed Sunday Mass. Missing was not even considered. And so, what
we learned about God from the experience of living with
our earthly father was that God the Father is steadfast, that
He will never leave us, and that He will always be there
for us.

The impression was so strong for me that when my
daughter was a little girl, the first thing I taught her was
something we called "the Rule". I would ask her, "What
is the Rule?" and she would respond, "No matter how, no
matter why, no matter when, no matter where, no matter

what, Daddy loves me." Then when she got a little older, I taught her the second part of the Rule, and she would recite, "And God loves me even more."

I taught her this rule as a reflection of what I had sensed from my father since my very first memories of life: unconditional love and affection. My father lived in a fashion that continually reminded me that there is nothing weak about showing kindness, concern, and affection for another human being; instead, such behavior is what makes a man a true man.

And it is this same kind of affection that led to my father's enthusiasm for the well-being of others. Sharing in the joy of others is one of the best kinds of affection we can offer—and it is the kind my father consistently gave to others. Throughout his life, he was giving and affectionate not only toward my brother, my sister, and me but also to each of our spouses, to all of our children, to his nieces and nephews, and even to his own brothers and sisters. He was also an unofficial godfather to many others—from partners at Goldman Sachs to kids who played football with my brother and me in Little League. And now, even their sons and daughters come to my father. And they come for two things: love and encouragement.

They would call and ask to come see him and say they wanted his advice. Many times—in fact, usually—they really did want his advice, but they also wanted his love and encouragement. In this Internet age, we can get advice from many places. But what is rare is to have someone you respect take time to encourage you, and when you have succeeded, to share in your joy.

Envy is one of the Seven Deadly Sins, but for some peculiar reason, my father seems not to have received his portion. He always used to say to my brother and me, when teaching us about negotiating and doing business deals, "Don't worry about how much money the other guy is putting in his pocket, as long as you are happy with what is going in yours." This is easier said than done. Jesus told the parable of the workers in the vineyard, who were happy with their wage until they heard that others earned the same wage for less work, at which point they became angry.

Jesus also had another story. He once cured ten lepers, and only one came back to thank Him. Interestingly enough, I think my father had a better "batting average" of gratitude shown him. It seems that most of the folks he has helped have come back to tell him of their successes and to thank him for helping them. And I think I figured out why they come back: I think they come and share their joy with him because they know that he will unabashedly share in their joy, without stealing any of it out of envy. This may sound like a trivial matter, but in the realm of human relations, it is not. Watch how often, when someone tells an interesting story, the person listening immediately wants to respond with an even better story, thereby stealing some of the thunder. Well, my father does not steal thunder—he provides an echo chamber for other people's thunder, and thereby increases their joy. He rejoices.

My father is a man of considerable accomplishment in this life, but the way he taught me about God was not through his accomplishments. He has taught me through steadfast loyalty, forthright love and affection, and sincere and enthusiastic encouragement that affirmed for me and for others that life is indeed a blessing, that each of us is indeed blessed, and that there is a God who loves us and affirms us.

# 13

# Chloe Langr

*Chloe Langr is a freelance writer, blogger, author, and editor. She is passionate about the feminine genius and women's ministry and is constantly inspired by Pope Saint John Paul II's Letter to Women. The love of her life proposed to her on the top of Emory Peak in Big Bend National Park, and they were married in 2017. When she isn't buried under a growing stack of books, you can find her climbing mountains, podcasting, and spending time with her husband, Joseph, and their daughter, Maeve. You can find more about Chloe on her blog,* Old Fashioned Girl. *Check out her two podcasts on iTunes,* Letters to Women *and* The Catholic Podcast. *You can also find out more about Chloe's passion for women's ministry in her book* Created for Love: Reflections for the Catholic Bride-to-Be, *published by Our Sunday Visitor in November 2019.*

Most kids don't know what their dads were thinking when they held them as babies. I, however, am incredibly blessed to know exactly what was going through my dad's mind during those first few months of my life.

On August 4, 1995, my dad sat down with a piece of lined paper and a pen and wrote down his thoughts in a letter to me. It was supposed to be opened on my sixteenth birthday. But letters can get lost easily in a house full of ten people—and then found again at exactly the right time. I ended up reading the letter right before I moved out of my parents' house after college. One part touched me more than any other, bringing tears to my eyes:

> While you are reading this letter, hopefully you are look-
> ing back over these years and have a smile on your face.
> Hopefully, your life has been good to you! Your mother
> and I want to be good parents. We will never give up on
> raising you. Growing up, I didn't have a good example of
> a father. But I will give you my all.

It wasn't until my dad was in his twenties that he found out that he had been adopted by his stepfather. His biological father didn't want to be involved in his life or the life of his family. When my dad discovered this, he was planning a life with my mom; it was about a year before they got married. I can't even imagine the heartbreak of not being able to share such a moment with my father.

If you gather research on what happens when boys are raised without their fathers, you'll find yourself sorting through some harrowing facts.

Boys who don't have a relationship with their dads are less likely to finish school and more likely to struggle with various addictions and be incarcerated—and that's just the tip of the iceberg. Emotionally and spiritually, these boys are more likely to struggle with depression, low self-esteem, and aggression.

It would have been understandable (and in keeping with research!) for my dad to become the same kind of man his father was. But instead of continuing a vicious cycle, Dad courageously took a stand for what he knew was right. He didn't strive to be the perfect dad—no one can fulfill that role but our Heavenly Father, after all. But he gave me, and the rest of my siblings, his all.

I'm my parents' first child, but I wasn't the last. My mom and dad had eight children during the first eighteen years of their marriage. My dad strove to lead each and every one of us to the Lord. He did this not by extravagant means but through simple, beautiful, tangible things that I still remember.

One family tradition was the 9:00 A.M. Mooradian family Rosary. As you can imagine, prayer time with so many little people running around was sometimes (okay, most times) the opposite of a quiet, peaceful experience. But despite our unrest or rowdiness, I remember my dad calmly sitting on the floor of my parents' bedroom, a rosary in one hand, a squirmy little person in the other. He encouraged us to add our own petitions at the beginning of the Rosary. He would often add in a prayer request for his marriage, his job, or the health of friends and family. When I was little, my dad worked the second shift at our local Hallmark greeting card factory, so he was with us in the morning before heading off to work. I will forever treasure the memories of starting our mornings with Dad, praying together as a family.

Another tradition my dad helped start in our family was a Tuesday-morning adoration hour together. My mom would corral us all into the car, and we'd drive to our parish adoration chapel. Even if my dad had to work in the morning (by that time, he had started his own pest-control service for extra income), it wasn't rare to see him pop in to the chapel on Tuesdays, if only for a few minutes, to say hello to Christ in the Eucharist and check to see how we were doing. When the Kansas weather was brutal, it was my dad who made the sometimes-treacherous journey to the chapel. He taught my siblings and me the importance of perseverance in prayer. I always loved to see him interact with the older women who prayed during the adoration hours before and after our hour. He took time to say good morning to them and ask how they were doing. My dad showed so much love for the Body of Christ during our visits to our little adoration chapel.

Even though we lived twenty-five minutes away from our parish, my family always made the effort to go to the 8:00 A.M. Mass on Sundays. As we would pull out of the garage and start the drive, my dad could always be counted on to compliment his wife and daughter on how beautiful they looked for Mass. I grew to appreciate this trait of my dad's even more as I became a teenager. My frustration over my unruly hair and my outfit were quickly forgotten thanks to my dad's kind words.

Once we arrived at Mass, we'd often see my dad stop in line for Confession before joining us in our pew. Seeing Dad would usually inspire even the littlest of us to join him in line. We loved beginning Mass with clean souls. We'd tumble over each other back into the pew and settle down into our places—yes, we each had a specific seat. We went over our seat charting before heading in to Mass. Certain siblings weren't allowed to sit by others, and other siblings did much better if they were sitting by my dad. By the homily, sometimes we'd look down the pew and see my dad fighting sleep, which would be met by little nudges from the kids sitting closest to him.

Looking back, I don't doubt that my dad was worn out by Sunday morning. He worked multiple jobs, started his own business, and later would go on to finish his bachelor's degree (even with eight kids running around the house)—all while supporting eight kids so my mom could stay home and homeschool us. But, despite his exhaustion, he still took our family to Mass, always leading us closer to the feet of our Heavenly Father.

"I also pray that you have a strong love for your Lord Jesus Christ", my dad wrote in that letter he penned when I was only a few months old. "This is where I hope that you are the strongest. This is the most important thing you can ever have—Jesus. We want you to have a great faith. You have such a rich history in faith. Continue to worship the Lord and support His Church."

Throughout my life, my dad has loved me with the love that reflects that of the Heavenly Father. As an undergraduate, I studied history at a college in my hometown. While writing my senior thesis, I put in countless hours at the library, pulling books from the stacks for research. During the last few weeks of the semester, everything started falling apart. After a grueling round of edits from my subject adviser, I realized that I was going to have to rewrite most of the thesis. Rejected and feeling like a failure, I went back to my parents' house (where I lived all throughout college) and sat down at my computer. Not long into the editing, the devil's lies begin to sneak into my heart: I'm not enough. I'm a failure. If I was any good at the subject I'm studying, this would never have happened.

Overwhelmed, overtired, and undermotivated, I began to sob, sitting in the family office chair. When Dad heard me, he came into the room and asked me how I was. Between tears and Kleenexes, I told him everything that was on my heart, and the lies that I was beginning to believe.

It would have been easy for my dad to dismiss my emotions, but instead, he sat with me and encouraged me. In my moment of frustration, he reminded me of my true identity as a child of God. He understood my frustration with my senior thesis but wouldn't let me call myself stupid or a failure.

Pope Saint John Paul II once said, "We are not the sum of our weaknesses and failures, we are the sum of the Father's love for us and our real capacity to become

the image of His Son Jesus."[1] It was that evening's conversation with my dad that gave me the motivation to
see past my failures and rejoice in my identity as God's
beloved daughter. But it wasn't just during that conversation my senior year of college: Dad's actions and words
have confirmed my identity as a child of God throughout
my entire life.

My dad could have easily followed the example his
father had given him when it came to parenting. Instead,
my dad's life is a story of a courageous redemption of
fatherhood. I never doubted that my dad loves me—and I
never doubted that he loves the Lord. He truly gave (and
continues to give!) my mom, my siblings, and me his all.

[1] Saint John Paul II, Homily at the Seventeenth World Youth Day (Toronto, Canada, July 28, 2002).

# 14

# Christopher Check

*Christopher Check is president of Catholic Answers, the Catholic world's largest lay-run apologetics and evangelization apostolate (Catholic.com). Before joining Catholic Answers, he served for two decades as executive vice president of the Rockford Institute, publisher of* Chronicles: A Magazine of American Culture. *Before that, he served for seven years as a field artillery officer in the United States Marine Corps. Christopher holds a degree in English literature from Rice University. He writes and speaks at home and abroad on Catholic heroes and villains and is the creator and voice of the Lepanto Lectures, a series of audio recordings on glorious and tragic events in Church history. Christopher and his wife, Jacqueline, have four sons, Nicholas, Alexander, John Paul, and Nathanael. The Checks breed and show Cavalier King Charles spaniels, famed companions of the Stuart Kings. Their kennel, Top Meadow Cavaliers, is named after G. K. Chesterton's Beaconsfield Estate.*

My father, Paul Check, is what the English would call "a man of parts": sailor and tennis player; gardener and chef; handyman and photographer; philosopher and nuclear engineer. He is an autodidact, a poet, a calligraphist, and a bibliophile. He designed elaborate Halloween costumes—in the third grade I was Odysseus, complete with greaves, breastplate, and helmet, all of *papier mâché*. Some of these loves, in his eighty-fifth year, Dad has laid aside, but not reader and not chef. To these two—books and food—in a moment.

With his extensive record collection—vinyl that came each month in the mail from the Musical Heritage Society—he taught my brothers and me what good music is. Bach and Mozart, Haydn and Handel played every evening on the family room's Heathkit turntable and amplifier, which Dad built at his basement workbench, with a white ashtray simultaneously holding a soldering iron and a cigar, and my older brother, Paul, at Dad's side, assisting with both.

Dad taught us what was art and what was not. There was no shortage in our home of books of the great masters through which to leaf, and on birthdays we passed on parties of kids amped on frosting and joined Dad in our '71 Buick Skylark for an excursion into the Federal District for an afternoon at the Smithsonian's National Gallery. My favorite was John Singleton Copley's *Watson and the Shark*, though for years I called it the "shark picture".

Above all, my father understood his role as a surrogate of God. His call was to form men like himself: whole men. He fulfilled this vocation, in the main, by example. On the outside we learned from him to dress in natural fibers: wool and cotton; silk for neckties; leather for shoes—soles, too. We learned to carry ourselves with quiet bearing. On this score, my brothers, Paul and Edward, paid closer attention.

Dad showed us what a life of service was—service to our neighborhood, to our parish, to our country. We joined our father in patching the neighborhood tennis courts and baking casseroles for the soup kitchen. Each day, we watched him walk to and from his post at the Bethesda office of the Nuclear Regulatory Commission, and sometimes we joined him on a Saturday at the office.

And we saw every day the central truth of a life of self-giving: the greatest example a father can provide his sons is his love for his wife.

To be sure, however, Dad's fatherhood included an active formation of his sons as well—a deliberate cultivation of the mind. He was clear: the truth exists. It is knowable. Love it. Conform your life to it. Why? Because it comes from God. In practice, this love of the truth grew in our hearts through reading and conversation, especially at the dinner table, where books and food converged.

My brothers and I grew up in a home full of books, books in every room. What was not available at 7810 Maple Ridge Road was just a few blocks away at the Bethesda Public Library. (Once there were such things as libraries.) I recall joining Dad on regular trips to the library and sometimes to a more distant branch in search of a volume that ours did not have, and I recall the perpetual stack of books on the round cherry table next to his Eames chair. Our father read late into the night, every night. He still does. Today, his own library, the fruit of more than half a century of collecting, fills his home. He must have nearly two thousand volumes.

To call my father's practice "collecting" is to do it a disservice. The word suggests a mere enthusiasm. Rather, building a veritable house of books, Dad helped create a world in which his sons would come face-to-face with their father's intention, whether in pulling a book off a shelf or simply in living life surrounded by good books. That intention was not what the world calls "success", or what the liars who have usurped today's academy call "searching". My father's intention was to impart the truth.

Again, the truth was real. It could be known. My father taught us to revere the truth and conform our lives to it.

Our home, however, was more than a library. Yes, we were surrounded by books, but our father followed through. Our home was a perpetual classroom—no, a seminar, and always accompanied by great food.

My mother, Dianne (and I'm looking forward to the book in which I can testify to her saintliness), may have a different version of events, but my memory is this: about the time that she went back to school to get her advanced degree in linguistics—was I in fifth grade?—Dad took over the kitchen, especially on weekends.

On a Saturday years later, tennis and gardening behind him, Dad was at the stove, and I was seated on the green kitchen stool. Seminar was in session. It was my senior year of high school, and I had been charged by my symbolic logic instructor to defend free will in a forthcoming debate. Setting down his wooden spoon, to the bookshelves my father went, gathering Aquinas and texts on apologetics and Christian doctrine. He hardly needed to, because he had all the defenses of free will in his head. How can we understand merit or fault, innocence or guilt, heroism or cowardice, outside of the context of free will? How long he must have waited for this moment, and to this day, I'm not certain he even knows what a watershed it was for me, but I was excited by the truth at that moment to a degree I had never been. The truth existed. It could be known. It should be loved.

Oddly enough, I don't recall what my father was cooking that afternoon or the dinner conversation that followed, but reflecting now on so many family meals, I understand why life at the dinner table in the Check house began so often with Dad's asking: "What book are you reading?" Over good food the conversation flowed, and as my brothers and I grew older, so did the red wine, and there was the Truth in our midst. It is something worth contemplating that when Our Lord rose from the dead, He did not reveal Himself in a blinding transfiguration or in the quelling of a tempest. He revealed Himself in the breaking of the bread, in the grilling of some fish, and doubtless, in the drinking of good red wine.

Scripture scholars may debate what Our Lord meant in Matthew 18:20: "There am I in the midst of them." We do know that good exegesis requires us to read each of the Gospels in the light of all four, so Matthew should be read in light of John, and it is in John, chapter 2, that Our Lord makes more red wine after the guests at Cana had already been well into the celebration. This warrant may be the only one in Scripture that my own sons have taken to heart, but, *Deo gratias*, it's a start. It is the patrimony I've handed down from my father, who understood that the right conversation and the right conviviality lead to the truth.

Dad understood that Our Lord appreciated a good party and one, it seems, that could go on for days—the custom for Jewish wedding feasts. Can you imagine the festivity at Cana as Our Lord and His apostles enjoyed a superabundance of the best red wine ever vinted? This was the life in which my brothers and I grew up—conversation and conviviality.

In Jackie's and my home there are books in every room. Three of our four sons are launched. They live together in a home in Saint Paul, and that home is the gathering place of all of their friends, a magnificent manifestation of Benedictine hospitality—my oldest son, Nicholas, at the stove. Whatever my sons do or will do to keep body and soul together is of less concern to me than this: that they all practice the faith. I take no credit. I did only what my father did. I cooked dinner. I started conversations. I told them that there was such a thing as the truth, that it was knowable, and that they should love it.

And in the course of those conversations, when they asked me how I knew something, I gave them the same answer my father gave me.

"I read books."

15

# Megan Collier Reilly

*Megan Collier Reilly is a stay-at-home wife and mother of four. She taught high school Spanish for eleven years, ten of them in Catholic schools in New Jersey, Rhode Island, and Massachusetts. She has attended two World Youth Days (in Denver and in Paris), studied abroad in Spain, and participated in two service trips to Mexico. She has done volunteer work at a Boston-area crisis pregnancy center and was a member of the Newton chapter of Massachusetts Citizens for Life, having had the honor of attending meetings alongside Dr. Mildred Jefferson, one of the greatest pro-life heroes of our time. Born and raised near Princeton, New Jersey, where she attended Stuart Country Day School of the Sacred Heart, she received her B.A. from Boston College and her M.Ed. from the PACT Program at Providence College. She and her husband, Mike, reside in North Kingstown, Rhode Island, along with their children: John (Jack), Daniel, Matthew, and Caroline. The Reillys are active members of their parish, St. Bernard's, and Megan continues to be an active participant in the Rhode Island pro-life movement. You can connect with Megan Reilly on Facebook (/megancreilly).*

It was the last speech he would ever give, and he knew he had to get it right.

Richard F. Collier Jr.—my dad—was being honored for his pro-life work yet again; this time, with the St. Thomas More Award given at a Red Mass by the Diocese of Metuchen, New Jersey. But he was not there for the

117

praise. In fact, just two months earlier, my mom and I had to plead with him to attend, as it would be rude otherwise! "How can I celebrate and party while babies are being murdered all around us?" he protested. So, on Sunday, October 27, 2013, Mom and I were pleased that we had convinced him to accept the invitation. What we couldn't have known was that he wasn't there because of us. No, Dad had always been in the business of saving souls, and that day was no different—except that it would be his last public appearance, his last great speaking engagement, his last appeal to us to protect and promote the culture of life, his last battle on this earth as a soldier for Christ. And so he fought.

To be there that morning required all the strength he could muster. Riddled with cancer after two and a half years (that we knew of), he explained in his speech that he had to stand long enough to take a shower, have help getting dressed, take his pain meds, and use a wheelchair for the first time. He almost didn't make it, and he mentioned all of this only to apologize in case he seemed to ramble. By the grace of God, he fought. He pulled himself up to the podium after Mass and held himself steady for twenty minutes as he delivered the speech of a lifetime to a crowd of family, friends, priests, colleagues, and fellow pro-lifers.

Beginning by quoting Oskar Schindler, "I could have done more", he called on us to be obsessed with our faith "because the other side is obsessed about persecuting us". He asked us to read or reread *Evangelium vitae* and get that "fire in our belly and do something", and he reminded us that the Church's core mission—our mission—is the salvation of souls.

He ended his speech in the same way he ended all of his conversations with his loved ones—by directing us to look at the example of the Blessed Mother, who was given the ultimate honor of being chosen to be the Mother of God. But instead of holding a press conference, he said, she went with haste into the hill country to help her pregnant cousin, Elizabeth. His last words to a captivated audience that morning could not have been clearer: "We members of the Church need to rise up and go with haste into the hill country, not only to help pregnant women and save their babies, but also to save the souls of those who are responsible for the culture of death in our society."

My dad was always spot-on with his predictions, which he shared with us so we would understand the situation and could prepare for what was to come. By November, he had predicted that he wouldn't make it until Christmas. So it was a shock to us all when my brother called us from the hospital around 3:30 on Christmas morning of 2013 to tell us that Dad had entered into eternal life. But we were able to rejoice. My first thought, because it is how my dad raised me to think, was "You made it, Daddy! You did it!" To us, there was no greater validation, no greater reward for a man who had spent his entire adult life fiercely fighting for the unborn than to be welcomed into Paradise on Baby Jesus' birthday, no doubt greeted by a choir of babies whose lives he had fought to save.

My dad was always working for the unborn, but more importantly, praying for them and soliciting our prayers too. One evening when I was in college, my dad called to ask me to pray for a fourteen-year-old girl whose parents were trying to force her to abort her child: "Please pray that I can help her, and please pray for her and her baby." I told him I would, and I did, and then got back to my own life. That same night, my dad called a pro-life colleague to ask if he would accompany him on yet another mission to save a baby. Their first stop was a judge's house around midnight to pick up a court order; by 1:00 A.M., they had arrived at the teenager's house. So eager was she to keep her child that she literally jumped out her bedroom window to sign the papers that moments later would be presented to her parents to prevent them from forcing her to abort. According to his colleague, my dad was "firm yet gentle in speaking to the father", who ultimately relented and stated that he would allow his daughter to have the baby. And the girl carried her baby to term.

At another point while I was in college, still blissfully unaware of the burdens my father was shouldering daily as a pro-life lawyer, a young mother was trying to make bail to abort her five-month-old baby. With three young children at home and arrested again on drug charges, she felt as if she could not handle the responsibility of another child. The judge who heard her case, though not pro-life and probably unaware of my father's pro-life work, simply believed she was too far along to abort and appointed my dad to represent her unborn child. He argued—fought—valiantly for the baby's life in front of another judge but lost, and the woman was released from jail to get an abortion, accompanied by her ACLU lawyer.

What happened next is amazing. She entered the abortion facility and then exited the abortion facility still pregnant. She emotionally embraced her mother and two pro-life leaders who had also worked tirelessly to convince her to keep her child. On Father's Day, her beautiful baby girl was born. My father's passionate description of what happens to a baby during an abortion and his plea on behalf of this unborn baby weren't enough to convince a judge, but they were enough to convince a mother. She said that listening to his words during the hearing is what convinced her to keep her baby.

The humble work in secret and suffer in silence. And so it was that Dad's family knew almost nothing about his pro-life work and these success stories until after his death. What we did know was that he was an overachiever and a perfectionist from the start, thanks in part to his Irish Catholic ancestry, his hard-working parents, and his Catholic education. Any goal he set for himself was always achieved, and he expected a lot from others because he first demanded only the best from himself. If ever there was a warrior for Christ you wanted on your side, it was Rich Collier.

The "fire in his belly" for Christ, as Dad often referred to it, was set ablaze in him at a young age. Every decision he made, action he took, relationship he formed, or word he spoke was rooted in his deep desire to please and honor the Lord. Ever the Boy Scout, he prepared for the rest of his life by ensuring that his conscience was properly formed in the faith at a young age. Receiving the sacraments frequently, attending daily Mass, praying the Rosary, spending time in Eucharistic adoration, and avoiding the temptations of the world were a part of his routine.

After excelling in high school, he received a scholarship to and graduated cum laude from Harvard, obtained a law degree from Boston University, and clerked for a federal judge in Trenton, New Jersey, at the start of his career as a corporate litigation lawyer. After much prayer and spiritual counseling, and many supplications to Saint Raphael, Dad determined that his vocation was to the Sacrament of Holy Matrimony. Knowing that this would be the most important decision he would ever make, he petitioned the Lord to help him find a woman who would be a good wife and mother, which he did when he met my mom teaching CCD at their local parish.

They married and started a family right away. My father made no secret of his love for children and his desire for a large family, but he happily accepted God's will as a father of three children on earth and three children lost to miscarriage.

As a teenager, he had become associated with Opus Dei. He credited the organization with helping him to tap into his sensitive side, thereby allowing him to be a more emotionally available husband and father and to find that delicate balance between disciplinarian and warmhearted dad.

The love and respect he gave my mother for thirty-six years served as an example when it was time for us children to pick our spouses. It was especially important for my brothers to witness the proper way for a man to treat a woman. Dad never raised his voice to Mom, he never uttered a disparaging word about her, and they never argued in public. He always complimented Mom in front of us, held her hand, and greeted her first when he walked through the door; and flowers on Valentine's Day (the anniversary of their engagement) were a must. One of the many preparations he made during his dying days was to have flowers arrive on my mom's doorstep on the Valentine's Day following his death—a final act of love and one last heartfelt goodbye.

In 1988, my dad and his partners opened their own law firm, Collier, Jacob & Mills. Over the course of thirty-six years as a lawyer, he rose to the top of his profession in the state of New Jersey, including serving as president of a county bar association, chairman of a New Jersey ethics committee, chairman of the Federal Practice Committee of the state bar association, a member of the Lawyers Advisory Committee for federal courts in New Jersey, and a member of the New Jersey State Advisory Committee of the U.S. Commission on Civil Rights.

In 1989, he became president of the Legal Center for Defense of Life, which provides legal defense and advocacy for the sanctity of human life from conception to natural death. Thus began his pro bono pro-life work, his ardent quest to save as many babies and mothers from abortion as possible, his tireless efforts to obtain justice for pro-lifers across the country, and his desire to change hearts and laws on abortion so as to ensure the protection of the inherent right to life of every person.

His library was filled with Catholic books by great theologians and saints, lives of the saints, commentaries on the Old and New Testaments, books on the true spirit and meaning of Vatican II, issues of *Magnificat*, and various encyclicals. He must have read every one of those books at least twice! He pored over the popes' encyclicals, especially those of Saint John Paul II, so that he was able to quote much of their content and often referred to them in conversation. He read constantly, whether it was his beloved theological literature, the *Wall Street Journal*, historical novels, the classics, or simply keeping abreast of the law, because he understood the power that lies in education, the pressing need for evangelization, and the dire importance of remaining one step ahead of the culture of death.

My dad was always loyal to his family, dedicated to his profession, and dogged in his defense of the unborn. He became an expert in First Amendment rights and cases and worked around the clock to provide legal expertise and representation at the drop of a hat. He never turned anyone away. Middle-of-the-night calls and car rides to judges' houses and interruptions during family vacations or holidays were commonplace. Even at the end of his life, knowing he was not long for this earth, suffering and in pain from his cancer, Dad always made time for the cause.

In 1997, he was hired by the New Jersey State Legislature to defend the Partial-Birth Abortion Ban, and he helped to write two amicus briefs filed with the U.S. Supreme Court to support the Nebraska partial-birth abortion ban case, decided in 2000. Both laws were struck down, but with the expert testimony he collected in the New Jersey case, Dad helped lay the groundwork for the federal ban on partial-birth abortion (2003) and the U.S. Supreme Court ruling in *Gonzales v. Carhart* (2007), which upheld the ban. He received many pro-life awards from state and national organizations, such as Legatus and the Knights of Columbus, was a speaker and lecturer at several universities and Rallies for Life on the steps of the New Jersey State House, wrote several articles for *Celebrate Life Magazine*, and was often mentioned and highlighted in articles and blog posts by Judie Brown of the American Life League. He also gave lectures advocating against embryonic stem cell research and defending traditional marriage and spoke on traditional marriage at Eagle Forum's annual convention in Washington, D.C., in 2006.

I don't know why some children fall away from the faith, and I don't think my dad ever took for granted that his kids wouldn't. He did, however, make our Catholicism as second nature to us as breathing and taught us from birth how to cultivate and maintain a relationship with our Lord Jesus Christ. Our house was Christ centered. There were crucifixes and holy statues in every room. We knelt by our beds for morning and evening prayers, said grace before each meal, prayed the Rosary and the Angelus, and said prayers before the Advent wreath. Mom and Dad read us Bible stories and the Baltimore Catechism each night when we were children, introduced us to books about the saints, and read from *Magnificat* on our way to Sunday Mass. No dirty language, movies, books, or television shows were permitted, and Dad spoke to us frankly about sin. Outside the house, we were expected to be just as holy and committed to

Christ, regardless of how embarrassing it sometimes was for us as teenagers or young adults to profess our faith in such an amoral society.

You can imagine what it must have been like growing up with a father whose role models were Saint Paul, Saint Thomas More (his all-time favorite), Saint John Paul II, Saint Josemaría Escrivá, and, as I recall, John Wayne. His motto, like Saint Thomas More's, was "I die the king's faithful servant, but God's first." He was a man of convictions. He was fair and just. He was unabashedly loyal to Christ, willing to defend the Church and her teachings anywhere, at any time, even if no one else around him would. He never separated his personal beliefs from his professional life in order to advance his career or his reputation. He hated the phrase "personally opposed, but ..." In fact, his refusal to set aside his religious beliefs in the public arena cost him promotions, prestigious positions, verdicts in his favor, and even friends and acquaintances. But another mantra of his was "For what shall it profit a man if he gain the whole world and lose his own soul?" (see Mk 8:36, Douay-Rheims).

Long before smartphones and Google, Dad would research locations and Mass times so we could attend Mass while on vacation. Nothing would stop us from attending Mass; we even drove the twenty minutes each way to and from Mass during many snowstorms.

From the moment we entered the church, always at least ten minutes early to pray, it was understood that we were there for the Lord. We were not to talk to our parents or each other. We genuflected, bowed before the altar, participated in the Mass, sang each song, received Communion reverently (after our hour of fasting prior to Mass), stayed after Mass to pray some more, and amazingly did all of this without Goldfish crackers or sippy cups.

We had been taught all of our prayers at an early age and knew the parts of the Mass, and our parents had explained to us the Real Presence of Christ in the Eucharist.

Our parents took us to Confession at least monthly, daily Mass whenever possible, and Eucharistic adoration. Whenever we passed by a Catholic church, we'd stop to pay a visit or at least bless ourselves. Dad sent us to Catholic schools, retreats, service trips, and World Youth Days in various countries. We even took a trip to Italy during the Jubilee Year and attended one of Saint John Paul II's Wednesday Audiences, with a place up near the altar.

In addition to all of these things, Dad followed in Christ's footsteps as best he could and was a true gentleman. He had this wonderful, self-deprecating sense of humor, along with a lighthearted remark for everything, such that one never knew how depressed and disturbed he was by all of the immorality in our society and all the sadness he felt when the courts ruled against life. Despite being one of the holiest men I have ever known, he would be the first to tell you that he was the most unworthy of Christ's great love and mercy. He worked hard to battle his inner demons, faults, and failings. Dad's preparation to meet Christ was no less intense on his deathbed, when he knew his time here was ending, than during the rest of his sixty-three years.

Dad was extremely generous with his charitable donations, frequently visited the sick and the elderly, was always present at major life events of family, friends, and colleagues, took great care of his parents and elderly family members in their old age, treated his professional adversaries respectfully, prayed and sought prayers for friend and foe alike, and was the ultimate peacemaker. I was the first of his children to be married, and Dad invited his more than fifty cousins, many of whom hadn't spoken to each other in over thirty years, due to various fallings-out from when they were only kids. Almost all of them attended and reconciled, and what a celebration it was! The joy on my dad's face that evening was priceless.

Dad took his vocation as a Catholic father quite seriously and helped to form us properly in the faith so that by the time we all left for Boston College and beyond, he could calmly let go and let God. We graduated, further pursued our education, and secured jobs that we hoped would make our parents proud. As young adults, we were so influenced by my parents' commitment to their marriage vows and parental responsibilities that we each decided upon the vocation of Holy Matrimony. On a family trip to Spain when my brothers and I were twenty-five, twenty-two, and nineteen, we stopped at a statue of Saint Raphael in the middle of Córdoba, where Dad fell silent to pray. (Afterward, he told me that he had been praying since we were babies for Saint Raphael to help us find good spouses.) Six weeks later, I met my husband.

By the grace of God, and certainly through the intercession of Saint Raphael, we found spouses who are also extremely committed to the Lord and to our vows to raise our children in the faith. And now, as we strive to be exemplary spouses and parents, we talk about Dad and what a secure, loving home and foundation he helped to create for us. It is our hope that we stay close to the Lord and our Blessed Mother and honor our own marriage commitments so that we, too, will provide our children with the joyful family life that we were blessed to have for so many years.

Thanks be to God and our Blessed Mother, we remain a close-knit family and are committed to carrying on where Dad left off in the pro-life movement. Even though we all miss him, there is no doubt that Dad had a hand in all of the joys we have experienced since his death. His legacy can be found in the commitment we have to ensuring that the Church's teachings and traditions are practiced and are passed down to his (now eleven) grandchildren and to future generations—a responsibility we take very seriously, and which is very rewarding as we watch our own children grow in Christ.

The Lord has an extraordinary way of bringing us comfort when we need it the most. At my father's wake, held providentially on the feast of the Holy Family, my family stood by his casket amid a sea of mourners as a woman approached with her sixteen-year-old daughter. It was the woman who had left jail to obtain an abortion, and with her was the baby she had given life to, now a beautiful teenager. When the mom heard of my father's death, she wanted to come to honor him and let us know how grateful to him she was for saving her daughter's life. We all embraced each other in tears as both women told us how much they loved my dad. It was a miraculous experience to be standing next to someone whose life your father had fought so hard to save. The strife was o'er, the battle done. Alleluia!

# 16

# Father Hezekias Carnazzo

*Father Hezekias Carnazzo graduated from Christendom College in 2004 and completed a master's degree in systematic theology with an Advanced Apostolic Catechetical Diploma at the Christendom Graduate School of Theology. In 2009, Father Hezekias founded the Institute of Catholic Culture and has since served as its executive director. Ordained to the priesthood on May 1, 2016, he also serves as pastor of Saint George Melkite Church in Sacramento, California, and as director of the Office of Catechesis and Evangelization for the Melkite Greek Catholic Eparchy of Newton. He and his wife, Linda, have seven children.*

On October 29, 1929, the American stock market crashed, and our economy crumbled in what would become known as the Great Depression. The economic crash of Black Tuesday had a devastating impact on society, as unemployment rose and families struggled to obtain the basic necessities.

It was in this financial and social environment that my father, William Salvatore Carnazzo, was born in 1933, the first of five children of Sebastiano and Fina Carnazzo. Sebastiano had recently graduated from medical school at Creighton University in Omaha, Nebraska. Finances were tight for this first-generation Sicilian immigrant, but the drive for the American dream was strong. It drove Sebastian and his brother to pursue the study of medicine, in hopes of a better future for their young families.

Ten years later, the Carnazzo brothers and their families had relocated to Monterey, California, and had established a family medical practice serving the Italian-speaking fishing community that was part of the sardine canning industry in Monterey Bay. With World War II driving an economic rebirth in the United States, and with the crisis of the Great Depression behind them, life was good for the Carnazzo family in Monterey. The good days would not last long, though. Unknown to most of the family, Sebastiano was suffering from a heart condition that would take him suddenly, leaving Fina and their five children without a husband and a father.

At twelve years old, my father, William, was thrust into a role of responsibility in his family that changed his life forever. From the world's perspective, my father's family was in crisis, but the eyes of faith offer a different perspective. As my father constantly reminds me, even today, "In everything God works for good with those who love him" (Rom 8:28). The psychological and economic challenges of helping to provide for the family at such a young age impacted my father deeply, and the hurt and loss of that time certainly left their mark on him. But the hand of the Lord was clearly guiding his character formation, and what emerged from the crucible of loss and hardship was a heart impressed with the generous love of the Lord.

In 1958, my father graduated from medical school, having paid his way through school with side jobs, being consumed by the same thirst for economic stability that had driven his father. By the time I was born in 1975, my father had, by all accounts, done quite well for himself. He was married, had a good job, owned his own home, and had three children. From the world's perspective, all was on track. One thing was missing, however. The constant economic concerns for his family had taken their toll, and following the path of so many in secularized America, he had wandered away from the Church. As a result, my brother and I, the youngest of our siblings, were not baptized, and we did not attend church as a family on Sundays. Soon the marriage of my parents, established as it was without a sure anchor in faith, was overcome by the disease of divorce, which tore my family apart in ways that cannot be described. The effects of the divorce of my parents still wound our family to this day. But again, "in everything God works for good with those who love him."

The divorce, and my mother's untimely death soon afterward when I was nine years old, shocked my father into asking serious questions about life and death. Through the evils that came upon my family, the Lord intervened and led my father through the "valley of the shadow of death" (Ps 23:4), bringing him back to the Church with a faith renewed by suffering.

Having lost his father at a young age, and now his wife and children through the evil of divorce, my father was left with nothing. It was here, in the depths of despair, living in a studio apartment in a physician dormitory, that he discovered the only one who could give him the security and hope he so desperately desired.

Although my father's return to the Catholic faith of his childhood was a slow, circuitous one, each stage of the journey (through "Bible churches", Christian businessmen's prayer groups, and Al-Anon meetings) was like a rung of a ladder that the Lord used to lift my father out of the perilous spiritual situation in which he found himself.

I remember clearly those days of my father's rediscovery of faith. But one of the most striking memories from those trying days was of one summer afternoon in which my siblings and I were allowed to spend the day with our dad (the divorce court had severely limited the time my father was allowed to be with us). As I remember it, the day was very hot, and we were driving through town with the windows rolled down. As we approached a stop sign, a large pickup truck pulled alongside our car, and the young men in it, a number of whom were riding in the back, shouted to my father, "Can we have a Bible?" My father pulled his car over, opened his trunk, and gave a Bible to each one of the boys. It was only then that I took the time to read and understand the magnetic sign that my father had placed on the door of his car: "Free Bibles. Just Ask."

Though this may seem insignificant to many, that moment had a great impact on the boys who called Dr. William Carnazzo their father. Over the years, my father's generous heart, that same heart that the Lord had prepared through many trials, became more and more evident to me. In my memory, not a day passed on which my father didn't give something to someone: a box of fruit after morning Mass to a large family in our parish; a used car to help some friend in a time of need; a pair of shoes to a less fortunate child; a room in our home to someone traveling through town.

The years following my mother's death were not easy for us. The divorce lawyers, eager to consume what little money was left, continued the court battles for years after her passing. Through this ordeal, my father's faith grew, and his heart was changed day by day. Although my father struggled continually with frustration and anger, the Lord, Who gave His life for us, became the model according to which my father determined to live his life. And passing this gift of faith on to his children was of the greatest importance. To this day, in times of frustration or difficulty in my life, my father reminds me to turn to the Lord and to His Blessed Mother, recalling the sweet words of the Memorare, which brought consolation to him in the most difficult moments of his life.

Though finances were tight—very tight at times—it was something my father had experienced before. And through all of it, he knew deep in his heart that "in everything God works for good with those who love him." At the end of each month, when my father's paycheck arrived, before bills were paid and lawyers were compensated, my father sat with us at our dining room table, and after discussing who needed help most, he asked us to write out the tithe checks ourselves, double-checking that the full tithe (10 percent) of his paycheck was given to the Lord. This lesson of returning to God a tithe of thanksgiving was, for me as a young boy, a lesson that had a deep impact upon my heart.

Today, after forty-plus years of my own journey of faith, I am thankful to my father for his example of generosity, which brought joy and freedom in the midst of sadness and loss. And it is that deep sense of life as a gift that has nourished me through my own struggles—giving me hope and joy in times of darkness. It is my firm belief that the trials my father faced throughout his life were part of God's mysterious plan, not only for him but for me as well. Through the difficulties and challenges of our lives, we discover our dependency upon the only one who can offer us hope, purpose, and true happiness.

My siblings and I were scarred by the tragedy of divorce and the loss of our mother. But the Lord's grace can heal any wound. By experiencing the generous heart of our father and his daily personal struggles, we learned that the Lord truly brings good out of evil and that generosity of heart can bring joy in the most difficult of circumstances. Following our father's example, my sister found her gift of service and love in the medical field as a nurse, often caring for the dying and the destitute. My brother and I accepted ordination to the holy priesthood within a year of each other, inspired by our father's deep faith and love for God's people. Today, whether we stand at the holy altar or at the bedside of the sick and the dying, we serve God's people with a love that was first revealed in Christ and was shown to us in the daily life and faith of our father.

Glory to God for the gift of my father's life, for his example, and for the faith that grows through the Cross of Christ.

*Remember, O most gracious Virgin Mary, that never was it known that anyone who fled to thy protection, implored thy help, or sought thine intercession was left unaided.*

*Inspired by this confidence, I fly unto thee, O Virgin of virgins, my mother; to thee do I come, before thee I stand, sinful and sorrowful. O Mother of the Word Incarnate, despise not my petitions, but in thy mercy hear and answer me. Amen.*

# 17

# Mary Rice Hasson and Jeanne White

*Mary Rice Hasson is the Kate O'Beirne Fellow in Catholic Studies at the Ethics and Public Policy Center in Washington, D.C. She also directs the Catholic Women's Forum, a network of Catholic professional women and scholars who seek to amplify the voice of Catholic women in support of human dignity, authentic freedom, and Catholic social teaching. Mary is an expert on topics related to women, faith, culture, family, and gender ideology. She speaks frequently at national, regional, and diocesan conferences and conducts workshops for Catholic parishes and dioceses on sexuality, gender identity, and pastoral care. She is the coauthor of* Get Out Now: Why You Should Pull Your Child from Public School Before It's Too Late *(Regnery, 2018), the editor of* Promise and Challenge: Catholic Women Reflect on Feminism, Complementarity, and the Church *(Our Sunday Visitor, 2015), and the coauthor with Kimberly Hahn of* Catholic Education: Homeward Bound *(Ignatius Press, 1996). Mary's sister Jeanne White lives in Michigan with her husband and family. She currently works for a nonprofit organization. She has devoted most of her life to raising her five children and volunteering at their schools and in her community to ensure that the values and example she learned growing up as a daughter of Charlie and Mary Rice would be passed on to her children. Jeanne's family is her greatest joy.*

This essay reflects on our father's life, not as hagiography— Dad wasn't perfect, and lived humbly dependent on sacramental grace from frequent Confession and daily

Communion—or even as biography, as our reflections are necessarily limited. We offer here the personal perspectives of two daughters, immeasurably grateful for our father and his influence in our lives, particularly his example of unwavering trust in God and love for the Church. In these reflections, we hope others, too, will hear the reassuring echo of his voice: "Trust God!"

## The Final Leg

Today I was informed by the University of Chicago that four biopsies on my back reveal a very serious melanoma that seriously reduces life expectancy. This e-mail is to confirm that I am placing this problem in the hands of Mary, our Mother, through the intercession of Fr. Walter Ciszek, S.J. I ask of Fr. Ciszek the grace of complete resignation to the will of God and the grace, if it be in accordance with the will of God, that this melanoma be cured. AMDG.

—Charles E. Rice, e-mail of July 10, 2014,
the day he learned he had terminal cancer

We've heard it said that how a person faces death reveals something about how the person has lived. So it was with our dad, Charlie Rice. The day he was diagnosed with terminal cancer, he wrote the e-mail above—and sent it only to himself. He knew then that, absent a miracle, the days and months ahead would bring an agonizing trial and an inevitable verdict. It's not that he feared death. He didn't. His whole life had been oriented toward his last "change of address", as he used to say with a wry smile—a homecoming joyfully anticipated.

But Dad loved his family, especially our mom, Mary. For our sakes, he asked God for more time. And he sought the

intercession of a saintly priest he had known years before—
Walter Ciszek, S.J.—who had survived the Soviet Gulag
and whose cause for canonization was pending. (Ever the
lawyer, Dad documented his intercessory prayer—if God
wanted to work a miracle through Father Ciszek's intercession, then Dad would do his part. But miracle or not, it
was all for the glory of God. Vintage Dad.)

Dad's note captures something about who he was: a
father and husband who met adversity with faith and faced
his mortality with unwavering trust in God and the Blessed
Mother.

On that day in July, Dad began the final leg of a lifelong
journey toward God.

## The "Double Whammy"

Within weeks of each other in early 2014, both Dad and
Mom had been diagnosed with cancer: Dad with melanoma, Mom with stage-4 lung cancer. They were in their
early eighties, and we were, frankly, more worried about
Mom. Her cancer was far more advanced, and she had
already battled serious lung problems and major surgery.
Dad, on the other hand, still did his Marine Corps calis-
thenics most mornings and ran on a track or a treadmill
three times a week. They were both tough, but Mom's
situation seemed more precarious.

We're not a family given to sentimentality or anxious
fretting—or self-pity. Action is a far better medicine.
(Long before Nike branded the phrase, Dad routinely
exhorted us, "Just do it.") The ensuing months were filled
with treatments and surgeries for both Mom and Dad. Our
family pulled together to help, supporting the local siblings, especially our sister Ellen, who lived with and helped

Mom and Dad. By early summer, it appeared that Dad's cancer was gone. Mom's treatments and follow-up tests continued; we weren't sure what lay ahead for her.

It was a shock to learn that Dad's melanoma had returned. He didn't share the prognosis, but we could guess, as he began aggressive, experimental treatment. The cancer spread. It was painful. Melanoma is an invading army, waging war on all fronts. To the casual observer, however, the devastation was hidden. Dad moved more gingerly and a tad slower than before but still "made his rounds"—to the law school at Notre Dame, to daily Mass, to his grandkids' school events, and of course, to his kids' homes. He still led the family Rosary, sometimes only with Mom and Ellen, but often with a houseful of sons, daughters, in-laws, and grandkids.

## Surrendering

In dying, Dad was still Dad. He bantered and joked. He read books and forwarded news articles or religious columns to kids and friends. He laughed out loud watching old TV shows, such as *Hogan's Heroes* and *F Troop*. And, for as long as he could, he did the dishes for Mom, as he had for years, and took care of the collies and cats who livened a house grown quiet without small children.

And he prayed, quietly and constantly. His faith was as natural and essential to his life as breathing. It was quite ordinary, in a sense. The man who urged us continually to "love God", "follow the Church", "go to Mass", "pray", and "trust God" also led by example, modeling trust and fidelity throughout his life. As his life on earth neared its end, he didn't waver, although he taught less by words than by example. There were poignant moments, of course, when grandkids left for college, work, or military service, unsure whether they would see him again. But the goodbyes were simple, ending with his usual sendoff: "Pray. Trust God."

Dad passed away on February 25, 2015, surrounded by family praying the Divine Mercy Chaplet. Months later, one of our siblings cleaned up Dad's computer files and discovered Dad's e-mail from that July day in which he entrusted himself completely to God and the Blessed Mother and sought the intercession of Father Ciszek. We were moved by but not surprised at his immediate, faith-filled response to his diagnosis and his trust in God and the Blessed Mother. It captured everything he had taught us throughout our lives. He fought the disease and fully accepted the will of God because he completely trusted Him. He surrendered to God—not only on July 10, when he learned his diagnosis but every day of his adult life, certainly for as long as we knew him. And because he loved God, he loved the Church. He knew the Church as God's gift, and he lived to encounter the living God through the sacraments. He embraced the Church's teachings as a sure guide illuminating the truth. God and His Church were inseparable in Dad's mind. He wanted us to love them too.

## Lessons Learned

So how does a father teach his children to trust God and love the Church? Our experience suggests these key takeaways.

*Put God first in your life.*

From our earliest years, we knew that Dad had his own prayer life and went to daily Mass. We'd glimpse him praying early in the morning and late at night. (With ten

kids, someone was always getting up at odd hours to use
the shared bathroom across from Mom and Dad's bedroom.) We'd tiptoe past and see him on his knees by the
bed or sitting, reading from a slim devotional. Every night,
he and Mom coordinated the next day's schedule; figuring
out which daily Mass to attend was always part of the conversation. We knew Dad said a Rosary while running—
because he suggested we do the same—and sometimes
while driving or even riding the lawn tractor on the
acres surrounding our home. Errands with Dad routinely
involved short detours, a few minutes to pray before the
Blessed Sacrament in the crypt chapel of Notre Dame's
Sacred Heart Basilica, or a brief stop to make a visit at a
nearby parish church.

Dad's example demonstrated that prayer happens any-
time, anyplace, as long as we put ourselves in the presence of God. He was attuned to God's nearness, blessing
himself or saying a quick prayer when passing a church.
When sirens sounded, he automatically led a Memorare
or a Hail Mary, asking Mary's intercession for those in
need. No matter how full his schedule, he made time for
a full hour of adoration at least weekly, often bringing his
legal pad along in order to think with God about whatever he was writing. For years, he joined a small group
quietly praying the Rosary in front of South Bend's abortion clinic. Sometimes we would join him, absorbing the
quiet lesson that prayer and personal witness matter, even
if it means sacrificing our desire for anonymity or our
wish to fit in. We learned that if we have the courage to
stand with God against evil, praying for His intervention,
He will work miracles.

Dad attended daily Mass throughout his adult life,
interrupted only when illness confined him to the house
or the hospital. He instilled in us the love of daily Mass,

mostly by example. He was strategic, however, in help-ing our desire to grow. He would nudge us out of bed early on Saturday to go to the seven o'clock Mass with him, even in the harsh South Bend winters, with the promise of doughnuts. Not just any doughnuts, mind you—Saturday morning Mass with Dad meant being the lucky ones with first choice of Fobe's West End Bakery doughnuts (truly the best!). When you are one of ten kids, having first choice of anything is rare, so the lure of the French cruller was often just the right incentive to get us out of bed on a weekend, to head for St. Joe's Church in Mishawaka. Once Mass started, we usually were happy that we had made the effort, even beyond the promise of doughnuts. As college students, we often met Dad at the crypt for daily Mass during the week, sometimes with a dining-hall doughnut or a chocolate bar for him as an after-Mass snack. In later years, a high point of visits home would be the chance to get up early to go to Mass with him. Those were treasured times.

In addition to prayer and the sacraments, Dad fed his spiritual life through daily spiritual reading. He gave us a steady stream of spiritual books too, such as the lives of the saints and *The Imitation of Christ*. Because his rec-ommendations came from his personal experience—often prefaced by, "Hey, I found this great little book"—we knew he used and valued these writings, and that was rea-son enough for us to read them.

In his final year, Dad devoted a great deal of time to praying—for Mom's health and his own, for their chil-dren, for a long litany of priests and religious, as well as friends and acquaintances in need of healing or other inter-ventions. Prayer was natural to him but not accidental. He had worked hard, mastering himself, to build habits of prayer over a lifetime. His spiritual leadership continued to his last breath: his final peace was rooted in his unwavering trust in God, nurtured through prayer over a lifetime.

*Spiritual leadership matters.*

Prayer was not only at the heart of Dad's day and central to his understanding of his vocation; it was also central to Mom and Dad's vision of what it meant to be a family. Dad's leadership was pivotal. He typically initiated family prayers, from the Morning Offering during our drive to school, to grace before meals and our family Rosary afterward. Family prayers every evening were nonnegotiable. (Dad made important concessions, however, for Notre Dame games, accommodating an evening kick-off by using the lengthy commercial time-outs for a decade of the Rosary.) While meals, playtime, and chores are the stuff of family life, the Rosary cemented a lasting spiritual bond among us. Years later, when first Dad and then Mom faced their final illnesses and eventual death, we automatically prayed the Rosary and the Divine Mercy Chaplet whenever we gathered at their bedsides. We were confident that they wanted us to pray together, and the Rosary united us spiritually with them and with each other in a beautiful way.

Family life provided opportunities for Dad to teach the faith and introduce us to new devotions and to the intercession of the saints. Family dinners included conversations about current issues, and Dad peppered us with questions about faith and how it applied to those issues. He also quizzed us on apologetics and history, with a quarter—later, a dollar—for any child who knew the answer. Our family said novenas to Saint Joseph to sell our house and other family property. We prayed to Saint Anthony for lost things and to Saint Gerard for Mom and our unborn siblings, and we sought the Blessed Mother's intervention for just about everything. Family prayers always included a litany of intentions for family and friends, for cures, new jobs, a friend's return to the faith, college admissions, and vocations. We prayed for help on our school tests and in our sporting events. In lean years, we prayed for money to pay particular bills or for God to supply our needs.

Don't imagine, however, that our family prayer time was typically—or even often—a pious, serene experience. It wasn't. It reflected the messiness of sin and the realities of life in a big family. Prayer time was not always reverent: behavior and cooperation fluctuated with children's ages, temperaments, and moods—and the family dogs were always a wild card in the midst of it all. Sometimes it was rushed. Sometimes kindness evaporated with an elbow jab from one annoyed sibling to another. Sometimes adolescent rebellion or teenage sulking cast a pall over it. No matter. We persevered. And Dad's constancy was the critical factor, staying the course in spite of potholes, speed bumps, and detours.

Over decades, we had learned to trust in God by seeing our parents' trustful turn to the Lord. They brought our family's specific needs—big and small—to prayer, always wrapped in deference to the will of God. Our parents consistently put our prayer intentions in context: we should bring our hearts' desires to God, but ultimately we must entrust ourselves—and every decision—to Him, confident that, as Scripture says, "God works for good with those who love him" (Rom 8:28). Over the years, we saw our prayers answered—sometimes dramatically, in the ways we hoped, and other times, in mysterious ways known only to God. As children, we saw and believed in the power of prayer and the providence of God because we saw God's hand in our lives and in the lives of those for whom we prayed. Our confidence and trust in God developed first through our parents' example and then through our own experience.

Dad's spiritual leadership also affected how we looked at our sins and failings (we certainly had and have many). When we struggled, Dad reminded us that we would see the path forward more clearly if we took care of the basics. Putting first things first meant prioritizing our relationships with God and doubling down on prayer and the sacraments, especially when we felt furthest from God. Dad's words had impact because this was how he lived. Sin exists, and we all fall, so repentance and Confession were woven into the rhythm of our family life. Dad would stand in the Confession line just like us, in need of God's forgiveness and grace. His example taught us to trust God not only to forgive our sins but also to give us the grace to do better.

A father's spiritual leadership is a tremendous gift to a child. When life was tough for us personally or for the family, we knew that Dad and Mom were praying hard, and we leaned on that immensely. Dad's exhortation to "trust God" came from deep within him—it seemed unshakeable—and that gave us great security, especially as children. He emphasized over and over that God is good and "in charge" and that His will is ultimately for our good. Even when we couldn't understand why certain things were happening, he encouraged us to trust God and to put anxiety aside. Dad's confidence in God was undeniable and inevitably contagious.

Perhaps it helped that we knew that Dad's assurances were the product not of an easy life but of a life walked with God, even through dark times. His own father had died when Dad was thirteen. He grieved the loss of his firstborn, who died in utero late in Mom's first pregnancy. He dealt with professional setbacks and political ridicule for his pro-life stand and his support of *Humanae vitae* and Church teachings on sexuality. He worked tremendously hard, laboring under the pressure of forming and educating ten kids on a professor's salary (back then, university salaries were quite modest). He suffered for us when, as teenagers and young adults, we took wrong turns or floundered under our weaknesses. We watched and learned. We trusted Dad, and Dad trusted God. Because of that, we learned to trust God. (Mom, too, was an incredible model of trust in the face of great difficulties—but that's a separate story!)

*Live generously.*

Generosity of heart nurtures trust. Self-pity kills it. We learned early on that a Christian gives of himself and his time, money, and resources, trusting God to make up for what he lacks.

Raising ten children during the high-inflation Carter years was tough. Money was tight. And after the *Roe v. Wade* abortion decision, Dad promised God that he would never turn down a chance to speak out and defend life. No exorbitant speaking fees—in fact, no set fees at all. Dad accepted whatever the sponsor could pay—even if it was nothing—in order to speak the truth about abortion and the value of life. Saint Paul wrote, "Woe to me if I do not preach the gospel" (1 Cor 9:16). Dad felt the same sense of urgency about life and its value. He told the truth, and he wanted people to know that abortion takes a human life. In pre-sonogram days, that fact was obscured by the rhetoric of pro-choicers, who dehumanized the unborn baby ("a clump of cells") at every turn.

Mom had an extraordinary talent for stretching a paycheck far beyond normal elasticity, but there were times when the question "Anything come in the mail?" would elicit worried shakes of the head, day after day. We'd pray together fervently that a check would come—to cover tuition, the electric bill, or whatever it might be. Dad's faith and trust in God exhibited itself in many ways, sometimes humorously. Many people will remember the turbulent economy in the mid-to-late 1970s. Gas lines, unemployment, and astronomical interest rates marked those years before 1980. Our family, like many others, struggled financially. Although Dad wrote and traveled extensively to speak, supplementing his salary, raising ten children was not inexpensive. Dad, however, approached it with his usual faith and humor. One night, a bill collector called our home, wanting to know when a certain bill would be paid. Without missing a beat, Dad said, "Oh, we're on the tri-payment plan." Confused, the woman on the other end of the phone said she had not heard of that plan. Dad's response, delivered in total deadpan and with a twinkle in his eye: "Well, you make one payment and try to make another." The bill collector hung up, no closer to receiving payment but hopefully somewhat amused.

Living generously meant welcoming children with joy. One memory is especially poignant. Mom became pregnant—at forty-five—with their tenth child during those tight financial years. My parents sold their one investment to cover maternity care and arranged for Mom to stay with close relatives in New York for the last few months of her pregnancy, to allow her to deliver under a specialist's care (she had a high-risk medical condition). Neither of them ever grumbled or regretted the financial sacrifice; they told us that they'd trust God and things would be fine. When Mom delivered our sister, Dad was miles away. (He was old-school, anyway, with no stomach for the delivery room.) But the day she gave birth, he was so thrilled that he decided to make the long drive to surprise her and see their new little daughter. The kids stayed with friends while Dad jumped in the car, drove all day from Indiana to New York, and walked unannounced into the maternity ward. Mom said later that she had heard his footsteps coming down the hallway and had the impossible thought, "That sounds like Charlie!" And it was! They were overjoyed—although Mom greeted him saying, "What on earth are you doing here? Where are the kids!?" It was a great moment for them both, sharing the joy of their new baby. Their joy was rooted in generosity, which, in turn, was rooted in deep trust. God would—and did—see them through.

For most of his nearly forty-five years at Notre Dame, Dad also volunteered his time—and his left hook—to coach students participating in the annual Bengal Bouts boxing tournament on campus. Even late in life, he enjoyed sparring with the students in the ring, teaching them physical and mental skills and toughness. It was for a good cause—to support the Holy Cross Missions in Bangladesh—and Dad loved being part of it. It was his way of giving while doing something he loved. Over the years, many students whom he had coached at Notre Dame made a point to stay in touch with Dad and visit when they were back on campus—to these young men, he was much more than a coach.

Dad and Mom's trust in God's generosity stood out in many ways. Not only was Dad a surrogate father to many Notre Dame students throughout the years, but on occasions far too numerous to count, he and Mom welcomed many students to family dinner, with only a moment's notice. During the holidays, our tables were always filled with "stray" students who had stayed on campus instead of going home. They were welcomed into our family because, with our parents, there was always room for one more. Mom was practical, though. Sometimes she would whisper "FHB", meaning "Family hold back" (no seconds and maybe limited "firsts" until our guests were fed). We loved having the students over; those dinners were always filled with laughter, and boisterous stories were told well into the night. The lesson learned? Sacrifices made with a generous heart can bring abundant joy.

*Love the Church.*

The Church is in crisis today, reeling from disclosures of child sexual abuse, cover-ups, and sexual misconduct by bishops and priests. We've been here before, though with different problems. In the turmoil after Vatican II, when nuns and priests left their vocations—and sometimes the Church—in droves, catechesis was replaced by felt banners and silly songs, and the hierarchy fell mute on contraception and extramarital sexuality, Dad taught us to love the Church no matter what. He reminded us that the Mass was the Mass, the holiness of the priest wasn't necessary for the Consecration to be valid (as long as the priest intended what the Church intended), and the magisterial teachings of the Church would not change because the truth doesn't change. And God doesn't change. God promised to guide His Church and keep her free from error, and Dad trusted in that promise. So do we.

Loving the Church had costs too, however. Early in our childhood, Dad and three close friends in New York established the Conservative Party of New York to counter the liberal ideology of the major political parties. Conservatism was hardly popular in the '60s, but Dad's taking an unpopular stance foreshadowed his courage in standing firm in defense of Catholic moral teachings. At Notre

Dame, Dad was a forceful voice in support of Catholic teachings on contraception, abortion, and sexuality. His biweekly columns in the *Observer* reflected a lonely reality: that there were many, even at Notre Dame, who didn't share the same love of the Church and her teachings. In the late 1980s, Dad joined in reciting the Rosary with his good friend Ed Murphy outside Notre Dame's Snite Museum of Art to protest the university's showing of the blasphemous film *The Last Temptation of Christ*. In 2009, he was among the faculty leaders who gathered for a peaceful Rosary protest while Notre Dame honored pro-abortion president Barack Obama with an honorary degree. A few years before he died, he braved threats and ugly protests at a Canadian university, where activists threatened him and tried to label as "hate speech" his talk on natural law and the Catholic faith. In his books, columns, and speeches, Dad did not shy away from unpopular stances in defense of the truth and the Church.

"Trust God" was always Dad's most important message to us. He knew that in all things we needed total trust in God's plans for us, even in facing death. Dad taught us that trust in God would strengthen us to accept God's answers to our prayers and to follow through, no matter what. It was this trust that always allowed Dad to stand up for what was right, and never be intimidated, and to face his illness and Mom's with his characteristic peace and optimism.

"Trust God" is more than shorthand for how Dad lived. It is his legacy—a truth he embedded in our lives. We are profoundly grateful.

# 18

# Father Gerald Murray Jr.

*Father Gerald E. Murray Jr. is the pastor of the Church of the Holy Family, the United Nations' parish, in the Turtle Bay neighborhood on the East Side of Manhattan. He was ordained a priest of the Archdiocese of New York on December 1, 1984. He has served at various parishes in the Bronx and in Manhattan. He studied at the Pontifical Gregorian University in Rome from 1993 to 1997 and was awarded a doctorate in canon law in 1998. He is a frequent guest on EWTN and the Fox News Channel and is a monthly columnist at the Catholic Thing website. He served as a chaplain in the U.S. Naval Reserve from 1994 to 2005.*

Gerald E. Murray, my father, died on September 1, 2017, at the age of eighty-six. He was a serious Catholic, by which I mean he treated his faith as the most important thing in his life. He believed that the doctrines of the Catholic Church are true and sought throughout his life to understand them better through prayer and study. He was an avid reader who loved the writings of John Henry Cardinal Newman and G. K. Chesterton. His influence on me as a boy and an adolescent was great. He inspired me to take my faith seriously. His example and that of my mother played no small role in my decision to answer the call to the priesthood. God's providential designs are often seen and appreciated only in hindsight. My father's death was an occasion to reflect back on his life and his influence on me and on so many others.

My father was born into an Irish Catholic family in Hoboken, New Jersey, in 1931. He attended Regis High School in Manhattan (class of 1949) and Saint Peter's College in Jersey City (class of 1953), both Jesuit schools. He served in the United States Army in Korea just after the truce was signed. Upon returning home, he attended Fordham Law School, another Jesuit school, and upon graduation in 1958, he married my mother, Mary Jane Moyles, one of only two female members of the morning section of his law-school class. In those days, the Jesuits had assigned seating at the law school, and Miss Moyles and Mr. Murray had been happily seated next to each other. The saying goes that, in real estate, what matters most is location, location, location. Perhaps my father had that thought in mind when he thanked God for giving him a last name that guaranteed a seat next to that of his future wife, an arrangement that his classmates might well have described as alphabetical discrimination. The Jesuits' seating plan was the instrument of some divinely ordered matchmaking at Fordham Law School.

Both my parents were always practicing Catholics, having come from devout families. They each received an excellent education in the faith, from the members of the Society of Jesus in my father's case and from the Religious of the Sacred Heart in my mother's case (the Convent of the Sacred Heart in Greenwich, Connecticut, and Newton College of the Sacred Heart in Massachusetts). Catholicism was at the heart of their marriage and their family. My two sisters, Margot and Mary Jane, and I learned our faith at home as naturally as we learned all the wonderful life lessons our parents imparted.

After their honeymoon, my father practiced law, and my mother stayed home to raise their three children. My mother later took up the practice of law when my youngest sister, Mary Jane, entered high school. My father worked hard and enjoyed his work. He loved the law. He said that he never had a bad day in the practice of law. That attitude toward the law revealed his gratitude for what the law means in the life of a society. The restraints and sanctions that the law places upon the human tendency to selfishness, greed, aggrandizement, and a host of other blameworthy behaviors are grounded ultimately in the divine law that calls us to live in accord with God's will. Truth, justice, and beauty are divine qualities that we must try to live up to if we want to live truly human lives that give glory to God and benefit others. My father saw the law as a bulwark supporting Western civilization's effort to keep the chaos produced by sin at bay by protecting what is right and just. When the law itself became an agent of injustice, as in the case of legalized abortion or the legal redefinition of marriage to include relationships based on immoral actions, my father saw the clear and present threat this posed to society.

My father was an early reader of *National Review* magazine and a fan of William F. Buckley Jr. and his circle of writers and thinkers. My father told me that the best autobiography of the twentieth century was *Witness*, by Whittaker Chambers, the former communist and Soviet spy who became a Christian and a champion of freedom against the monstrous communist tyranny and its agents in America. After reading *Witness*, I agreed. My father was a member of Neil McCaffrey's Conservative Book Club. He regularly received in the mail the club's monthly offerings, which I was delighted to peruse.

When I was a high school student at Regis, I would take the train into New York City with my father from our home in New Rochelle, New York. My dad was an avid reader of the *Wall Street Journal*, especially the editorial pages. He would regularly pass me the carefully folded paper so I could read Irving Kristol's columns and other outstanding pieces. Dad was educating me to take seriously the battle of ideas that was being waged in defense of the philosophical foundations of both the Church's doctrines and the premises of our civilization. He taught me that the truth is permanent and unchangeable and that it needs defenders if it is to remain the inspiration of our laws and societal customs. Freedom is God's gift to man, but the enemies of freedom are always at work to coerce man into submission to the vain pursuit of one or another false worldview.

My father lived his faith day in and day out. I remember the day I learned that my father attended daily Mass. I was in first or second grade, and I was stunned. I told him that we only have to go to Mass on Sundays. He told me that he liked going to Mass during the week. He loved to receive Holy Communion more frequently than once a week. When he worked in the Wall Street area, he would go to the parish of Our Lady of Victory on the corner of Pine and William Streets, near Federal Hall. He would also go to Confession there, as did so many others in those happy days of widespread practice of the faith by Catholics of all ages. Catholicism was considered a thing to be lived and enjoyed, not simply an idea to be thought about occasionally when things went badly.

At my father's funeral Mass I preached about his deep faith. Below is a transcript of that homily.

Ǝ❧

In the preface of the Mass of Christian Burial the Church prays: "Lord, for your faithful people life is changed, not ended. When the body of our earthly dwelling lies in death we gain an everlasting dwelling place in heaven."

Life is changed not ended. This truth of our faith is based on Christ's promise that those who are faithful to Him on this earth will be with Him forever in Heaven: "Come, O blessed of my Father, inherit the kingdom prepared for you from the foundation of the world; for I was hungry and you gave me food, I was thirsty and you gave me drink, I was a stranger and you welcomed me, I was naked and you clothed me, I was sick and you visited me, I was in prison and you came to me'" (Mt 25:34–36). Our Lord welcomes in Heaven those who have served Him faithfully on earth.

But to serve our unseen God in holiness and truth requires that we have faith in Christ, who walked among us two thousand years ago and continues to be with us through the power of His grace. We must all fight the good fight of faith against spiritual laziness, doubt, and any temptation to disbelieve. We must stake our lives on the truth of Christ's words: "I am the way, and the truth, and the life" (Jn 14:6). It is not enough to know that Our Lord said these words, or that others believe them to be true, or that they have inspired the saints to do great things for God throughout history. No, what is required of us is that we take these words as the guiding principle of our entire lives. As Robert Cardinal Sarah told us in his inspiring book, we have only one choice in life: God or nothing.

My father was a lifelong, grateful student of John Henry Cardinal Newman. I remember as a boy asking him about a book he was reading with the curious title *Apologia Pro Vita Sua*. Newman's defense of his life against his critics, my father informed me, was a masterful work of a spiritual giant. My father looked to Newman for enlightenment, guidance, and inspiration.

Regarding faith, Newman said: "Faith is the result of the act of the will, following upon a conviction that to believe is a duty."[1] Faith is duty because we owe the One Who made and redeemed us the homage of loving obedience, ever seeking to know His will and to put it into practice. A mind enlightened and strengthened by grace and convinced of the truth of Christ happily has only one path to follow: Christ, the Way, the Truth, and the Life.

My father was a serious Catholic. His joy as a believer was rooted in the solidity of the Church founded on the rock, and on the unchanging teaching of Christ. That doctrine taught him what to love in this world, and what to turn away from as displeasing to the Lord. My father believed and lived his faith with the naturalness of a true son of God.

He benefited greatly from his eleven years of Jesuit education. He often said that he owed the Jesuits at Regis High School a tremendous debt of gratitude for the spiritual, intellectual, and moral formation he received. He was a guard on the 1948 undefeated varsity basketball team. He was an actor in the drama club. Both of these activities prepared him well for his life as a husband, father, and lawyer. He knew what teamwork meant. He appreciated persistence in seeking to achieve a goal. As regards acting, he was fond of quoting George Burns, who said: "Sincerity—if you can fake that, you've got it made." Dad had no need to fake sincerity. He knew that there are many ways to present honestly a winning argument when the point at issue was worth arguing for. He was kind and patient and mild. He lived

---

[1] Newman to Mrs. William Froude, June 27, 1848, in *The Life of John Henry Newman: Based on His Private Journals and Correspondence* by Wilfrid Ward, vol. 1 (New York: Longmans, Green, 1912), 242.

according to Cardinal Newman's well-known description of a gentleman:

> Hence it is that it is almost a definition of a gentleman to say that he is one who never inflicts pain. The true gentleman ... carefully avoids whatever may cause a jar or a jolt in the minds of those with whom he is cast—all clashing of opinion, or collision of feeling, all restraint, or suspicion, or gloom, or resentment; his great concern being to make every one at his ease and at home.[2]

This gentlemanly graciousness did not mean that he was a pushover. I remember once, in my youthful argumentativeness, attempting to refute something my father said with the remark: "Dad, that is something out of the Middle Ages." To which he calmly responded: "What's wrong with the Middle Ages?" On later reflection, I saw not only that Dad was right but that he was trying to get me to think reasonably, avoiding recourse to facile slogans that are nothing but substitutes for thought.

Newman said: "Yet nothing is more common than for men to think that because they are familiar with words, they understand the ideas they stand for."[3] Dad was a man who knew the meaning of words, of the ideas conveyed by those words, and of our need always to seek the truth, because that is what brings us closer to God and thus to one another.

Newman describes the gentleman as someone who "never speaks of himself except when compelled, never

[2] "The Man of the World", in *Selections from the Prose Writings of John Henry, Cardinal Newman*, ed. Lewis E. Gates (New York: Henry Holt and Company, 1895), 16.

[3] Sermon 4, "Secret Faults", in *Plain and Parochial Sermons* (San Francisco: Ignatius Press, 1987), 31.

defends himself by a mere retort; he has no ears for slander or gossip, is scrupulous in imputing motives to those who interfere with him, and interprets everything for the best."[4] My family and his many friends were the beneficiaries of my father's fidelity to this Christlike way of dealing with his fellow man.

In considering my father's life, I would like to quote Cardinal Newman's brief essay "A Short Road to Perfection": "It is the saying of holy men that, if we wish to be perfect, we have nothing more to do than to perform the ordinary duties of the day well. He, then, is perfect who does the work of the day perfectly, and we need not go beyond this to seek for perfection. You need not go out of the round of the day."[5]

My father knew how to fill his days with ordinary duties performed with excellence, with love for God as the motivating cause. May he now receive the reward of his labors; may our prayers, if need be, assist him in completing that journey to the land of the living where we look forward to being with God forever, as Cardinal Newman so beautifully described: "After the fever of life; after wearinesses and sicknesses; fightings and despondings; languor and fretfulness; struggling and failing, struggling and succeeding; after all the changes and chances of this troubled unhealthy state, at length comes death, at length the White Throne of God, at length the Beatific Vision."[6]

≥♥

[4] "Discourse 8: Knowledge Viewed in Relation to Religion", in *The Idea of a University: Defined and Illustrated* (New York: Longmans, Green, 1905), 209.

[5] "A Short Road to Perfection", in *Meditations and Devotions of the Late Cardinal Newman* (New York: Longmans, Green, 1903), 285.

[6] *Parochial and Plain Sermons* (San Francisco: Ignatius Press, 1997), 1416.

What I most admired about my father was his combination of great patience with our human weaknesses and foibles, and his immoveable attachment to the truths of the Catholic faith. He always stood his ground as a Catholic when others turned aside from the faith to embrace errors and fads and in the process dismissed people such as my father as wrongheaded or uncaring conservatives. He felt sorry for them, not angry. He knew well the life of the Church before the Second Vatican Council and lived most of his life experiencing the turmoil that followed in the wake of that council. The Church is the Mystical Body of Christ, and her doctrine is Christ's doctrine. Those who sought to revolutionize the Church were misguided people acting on profoundly deficient philosophical and theological assumptions. Their errors would produce much trouble for the faithful, but the faith always remains the same. My father taught me this by word and example. He knew that Catholicism, ever under assault, is always victorious, even when its enemies seem to prevail.

My father would pray devoutly in his last months as he suffered the complications of Parkinson's disease. It was my privilege to bring him Holy Communion at home and see him receive Our Lord with the unaffected piety of a child. I am sure he made his First Holy Communion with that same devotion. He encouraged me to stand firm in the face of disorder in the Church and to trust in God's providence. He knew that providence had guided and carried him his whole life, and he was truly grateful for that.

Looking for Christ day in and day out, finding Christ day in and day out, right up to the moment when Christ calls us to Himself: this is what it means to be a serious Catholic. My dad was just such a man. I pray that I will follow his example right up to the end.

19

# Nancy Perkins

*Nancy Perkins has been married for almost thirty years to her husband, Charlie, and has two adult children, Jake and Rachel. Being their mom is her favorite job, but Nancy has also worked at Michigan State University since 1987 in finance. She is a member of St. Joseph Catholic Church in Saint Johns, Michigan.*

We all know the importance of a mother in a child's life, but I believe that the positive impact a father can make in the life of his children is often undervalued. A good father is the leader of a family, loves and respects his wife, and directs his children to their greater Father—God. This was my dad.

One of my earliest memories with my dad was our Sunday mornings together. It was always the same; my dad made a big breakfast and asked me if I wanted some. I always told him no but then proceeded to sit on his lap and eat all of his. After breakfast, we headed to Mass. Wanting to be just like my dad, whom I loved and admired so much, I mirrored what he did during Mass. I could see how deeply moved he was during the hour or so that we were there, and how he was spiritually touched by different parts of the Mass. I believe this early memory set the tone for how I wanted to live my life. Sometimes people act one way during a church service and then act quite differently once the service is over. This was not the case with my dad.

So many times I observed my dad do the right thing, and he did so with his actions more than with his words. I remember my mom telling me that when they dated, they always had their dates in public and often with other couples. My mom lived in an apartment at the time, and the only time my dad entered her apartment was to help her move out when they were getting married. I believe he did this because he had the utmost love and respect for my mom and because he was acting in faith for the Church he loved and believed in. He avoided any situation that could cause dishonor. He lived the faith.

I remember my dad coming home after a long day of work in the automobile factory when I was a little girl. It was the best part of the day because when he stepped out of the car, his children were his number-one priority— not watching TV or reading the paper or eating dinner or anything else. He would get out of the car and come right to us kids to play with us, read to us, and hear about our day. A short time later, we would eat dinner *as a family.* Prayers always came first; then we shared our dinner and stories about our day. He lived the faith.

In 1978, my mom was diagnosed with stage-4 breast cancer. The prognosis at the time was not good. The doctor shared this with my dad, and my dad asked the doctor not to let my mom know the prognosis. She knew she had breast cancer, but my dad wanted her to have hope and feel as if she had a fighting chance. I will never forget the day my dad shared this news with us kids. I remember him standing in the doorway to the dining room; "Your mom has breast cancer," he said with tears in his eyes. I will never forget the pain I felt for all of us. It was years later that my mom's oncologist shared with her what my dad knew. He was protecting his family, as a father should. I am so happy that my mom beat the cancer and lived to be eighty-three. My dad lived the faith.

Throughout his life, my dad volunteered in our community. He worked many hours for our local VFW, delivered for Meals on Wheels after he retired, and volunteered in our church and our church cemetery. He did all of this not to be recognized but because he had such a giving heart and wanted to help others. He wanted to be like Christ. He lived the faith.

Something my dad passed on to all of his children was contentment. He never wanted the fanciest car or the fanciest clothes. He was fulfilled by his family, and he was living his life with the ultimate goal in mind: eternity in Heaven for all of us. He lived the faith.

In 2008, after a short battle with pulmonary fibrosis, he transitioned from earth to his heavenly home. His passing on to Heaven was the most beautiful thing I have ever experienced. The peace he had in knowing where he was going is something that will live with me forever. With my mom, all of his kids, our spouses, and his grandkids by his side, he left this earth on December 19, 2008. He said goodbye to each of us, said, "I love you all", and closed his eyes. We knew where he was going because he had lived the faith.

During his funeral Mass, my sister felt her phone vibrate in her purse. She was a little surprised that someone would be calling her during Dad's service. Afterward, she found there was a message on her phone: "Hi, this is your dad," said the male voice. "I wanted to let you know I made it home." The caller obviously had the wrong number, but the message was clear. My dad had completed his journey to Heaven and wanted us to know. We never had a doubt, Dad.

Not a day goes by when I do not think of him and the wonderful example he set for his children and grandchildren. We were blessed beyond measure to call him our father and grandfather. My mom joined my dad in Heaven on March 1, 2019. She, too, was at peace, knowing where she was going to spend eternity. On her last day, she told her children, "I'm getting married today." I know Dad was waiting for her.

I think of my parents every day. We were blessed to have a wonderful example of how Jesus intended a husband and wife to live.

Now, because of our parents, we live the faith.

# 20

# Matt Birk

*Matt Birk is a Catholic, husband, father, fifteen-year NFL vet-
eran, 2011 NFL Man of the Year, and 2013 Super Bowl champion. He is involved in many causes for the Catholic Church.
He declined an invitation to the White House in 2013 based
on then-President Obama's "God bless Planned Parenthood"
speech. Matt is CEO of Matt Birk and Company, an organization that specializes in keynote speeches, business consulting, and
presentation coaching. He is cofounder of Unity High School, a
Catholic high school in the south metro of the Twin Cities that
seeks to develop virtuous leaders with real-world skills. Matt and
his wife, Adrianna, reside outside Saint Paul, Minnesota, with
their eight children.*

Robert John Birk was born on July 5, 1946. The second
oldest of seven children, my dad grew up on the East
Side of Saint Paul. Home to a couple of breweries and
more than a couple of bars, the East Side was as blue col-
lar as it gets. My father has a saying: "The East Side is a
good place to be from"—meaning, "You don't want live
there now."

My dad's mother died when he was just thirteen years
old. His father worked long hours at a local car dealership
in order to support his family. Since my dad was the oldest
son, he not only had to fend for himself but also learned
naturally to protect his siblings. Over the years, I've heard

from my uncles at family gatherings that my dad took his role as protector and enforcer very seriously, and that he was pretty good at it. I don't doubt it for a minute, but my dad would never tell you the same. It isn't his style to brag, and I'm not sure he thinks that being a good fighter is necessarily a source of pride.

In 1966, my dad was drafted into the Army. He was sent to Vietnam for two tours of duty at the height of the war. He doesn't talk about it, ever. The only time I asked him about his service was when I was writing a report in high school. My dad opened up for about five minutes. He didn't go into much detail, but I know he saw real combat, and I know that it affected him at the deepest level. I can't begin to envision what that was like, and I can't imagine how something like that wouldn't change a man.

The first job I remember my father having was that of a traveling camera and film salesman. Now and then on a Saturday, he would take my two younger brothers and me into the office with him. Going to work with dad was cool, but the vending machines in his building were our main source of attraction. We thought they were amazing!

My father is very affable and is a great conversationalist. A voracious reader, my dad is smart and wise. He genuinely enjoys talking with people, so he is a natural salesman. But with three sons born within the span of four years, he knew that being on the road wasn't conducive to our family. So my dad did what he needed to do: he quit his job so that he could be home with us more. I remember my brothers and I were bummed because that meant that attending the company picnic, the highlight of our year, would cease forever. At first glance, our reaction might seem ridiculous, but since we never had enough money to go on vacation, that summer picnic was like Disney World to us.

My mother had a solid job, with benefits, working at a nursing home, so my dad worked his schedule around her career. For fifteen years, he delivered newspapers. My father didn't have a single paper route; he had about ten paper routes. He would get up at 3:00 A.M. and head out—7 days a week, 365 days a year. That's my dad. No glamour, no fanfare; he just went to work every day and got it done. My mom would leave for work at 6:00, and Dad would be back from his paper deliveries around 7:00. He would make our lunches and get us off to school. During the day, he would pick up odd jobs. After school, the afternoon papers had to be delivered, and my brothers and I would help out. Honestly, I don't know how much help we provided. But the example was set: both of our parents were workhorses and showed us boys what a strong work ethic looked like.

During his high school years, my dad attended Nazareth Hall, which, until 1970, was a seminary prep school. Luckily for me, he didn't continue down the path to the priesthood. He is, however, a man of deep faith. Though we couldn't afford it, he and mom found a way to send my brothers and me to Catholic schools for all twelve years of school. Dad instilled in us respect and honor toward God. No matter where we happened to be when Sunday rolled around, we went to church. Never once did we miss Mass growing up. And every night, Dad knelt down with us next to our beds, and together we said our prayers. That's my dad.

By his actions and example, he taught us that Christ is within every person we encounter. My mom and dad regularly served meals as volunteers at the Dorothy Day Center, a homeless shelter in Saint Paul. They included my brothers and me in this service to those less fortunate. It didn't feel as if they or we were doing anything extra; it's just what we did.

Even though my dad spent a lot of time working to support us, he was always present and involved in our family. He coached our baseball teams and is a true lover of the game. I bet my dad and I played catch at least a million times growing up. Never once did he say no or that he was too busy when I asked. That's my dad.

As a coach, my father was great because he's very patient and has great perspective. He wasn't one of those parents who thought his kids were going to play in the pros. My dad just wanted kids—both his sons and those he coached—to have a good experience and enjoy the game that he loved so much. The competitive, overzealous (some might say "crazy") parents irked him so much that he became commissioner of the youth baseball league, in order to make a difference and offer the players a better example. I remember our dining room floor being covered with piles of registration forms—his personal system for putting the teams together. Our home phone would ring constantly with calls from parents who had special requests. He listened, considered, and then did what he thought was best for the kids.

My father didn't mind letting parents and spectators know when they were out of line and needed to calm down. He is pretty easygoing for the most part, but he has an intensity that serves him well. Whether you were a member of the team or a member of the family, if my dad was upset with you, you knew it. He didn't have to say a word. Trust me, I know. Dad let us make mistakes, and if we broke the rules, we suffered the consequences. He never really sat us down and had big, long talks with us, but he had a way of getting his point across. That's my dad.

I struggled in my freshman year of college. School and football had always come easy to me, but my first semester at Harvard was a disaster. For the first time in my life, I had to fight to make any headway in the classroom and on the football field, and it shook me. I didn't think I could do it. I was ready to quit and settle for the easy course. When I came home for Christmas break (my first trip home since leaving for college), I had made up my mind that I wasn't going back. My plan was to transfer to the local university so I could be back in my comfort zone with my high school mates. I packed up everything I owned (which wasn't very much), vowing never to return to Cambridge. When I finally worked up the courage to tell my parents of my new direction, my dad was quiet for a few seconds (it seemed like an hour) and very matter-of-factly said, "No, you're going back." And that was the end of it. I knew better than to try to plead my case. I could tell that he wasn't going to change his mind. That's my dad.

A few weeks after I returned to campus, I received a letter in the mail from my dad. He told me that I should realize how fortunate I was to be attending a great university with the opportunity to play a sport that I loved. Dad juxtaposed my situation with what happened to him when he was my age: he was given a trip to Vietnam, with no guarantee of a return flight. I can't tell you the shame I felt when I read Dad's letter. His intent wasn't to make me feel bad about myself; rather, he was giving me a healthy dose of perspective. In that instant, my whole outlook on life changed. My dad has an ability to strip away all confusion and distractions and cut right to the heart of the matter. He doesn't get caught up in anything but the facts and the truth. That's my dad.

Though I might have come far in life, my father knows his job isn't done; he is still guiding and directing me, helping me to become a better man. And that's my dad. Thank God.

# 21

# Father Francis Hoffman (Father Rocky)

*Reverend Francis J. Hoffman (Father Rocky) has been serving as executive director and CEO of Relevant Radio® since 2010. Relevant Radio broadcasts on more than 170 AM and FM stations, reaching 41 states and 220 million persons. Ordained as a priest for Opus Dei in 1992, Father Hoffman is a noted author and speaker and has appeared on the major radio and television networks. He has a B.A. in history from Northwestern University, an M.B.A. from the University of Notre Dame, and a doctorate in canon law from the Pontifical University of the Holy Cross. Prior to his assignment at Relevant Radio, Father Hoffman was chaplain of Northridge Prep School in Chicago and served in the rural highlands of Michoacán, Mexico, for fifteen summers. Before becoming a priest, Father Hoffman worked in sales for Inland Steel Company and later in tax and audit for Crowe Chizek and Company, CPAs.*

I never met my father's father, but I was named after him—Francis Joseph Hoffman. Grandpa died in 1939, and I was born twenty years later. The story is told that my mother wanted to name me Peter (that's where my nickname, Rocky, comes from), but my father wanted to honor his father by having me—the youngest of eight children—christened with his father's name. And so I was.

I am a Catholic priest. I have no children of my own. So I cannot honor my father by passing on his name. But I can honor him—and I am very happy to do so—by writing this chapter about him and how he influenced me, for the better, to know and love the faith that I profess.

Growing up in the '60s and '70s in a small town north of Chicago, I was surrounded by and immersed in the Catholic faith just about everywhere I went. There were a thousand students in our Catholic grade school. Our family attended the 10:00 A.M. Mass every Sunday at Santa Maria del Popolo. Most of the parishes in and around our town were named after Our Lady: Santa Maria del Popolo, St. Mary of the Annunciation, St. Mary's in Lake Forest, St. Mary of Vernon Hills. There was a road named St. Mary's. The largest seminary in the United States, Saint Mary of the Lake, was in our town. Its magnificent chapel of perpetual adoration is named Marytown. Even our town, Mundelein, was named after a cardinal. I think the first time I can remember encountering non-Catholics in our town was when I started playing Little League baseball and football. They seemed like good folks to me.

Even surrounded by good, serious, practicing Catholics, I had a sense that my parents were a bit more engaged in the faith. We always said grace before meals. Ours was the only house on the block with a nativity scene in the front yard at Christmas. It took a lot of work to build that crèche, cobbled together with five or six sides of wooden shipping containers from my father's shop and accented with real hay. It was a lot of fun working on that project with my dad. Reflecting on that tradition now, decades later, I think maybe that was my father's way of speaking Joshua's words: "As for me and my house, we will serve the LORD" (24:15), or maybe it was his way of imitating Saint Joseph the Worker, whose statue, complete with a leather coverall and hammer, graced our parish church.

My father made sure the Hoffman kids always turned in their collection envelopes on Sundays at Mass, and if we had no money left over from our allowances, our father would give us some money to pitch in. He always seemed to be giving. After he joined the Knights of Columbus, he would volunteer at the Veterans Affairs hospital at the Great Lakes Naval Station one Sunday a month, to help wheelchair-bound veterans get to Sunday Mass. When I started to frequent a center of Opus Dei in high school, he would always give me ten bucks—a lot money in those days—to pitch in to help support their work. Dad was a generous man: tips at the restaurant, handouts to beggars on the street, gifts for birthdays and Christmas. He modeled this generosity for his children, and he took the extra steps to encourage and enable us to be generous. He wanted to make generosity a habit that would be hard to break, and he was successful.

His generosity was something far greater than civic virtue. His "city" was the Church. It was as big as all of Heaven and all of earth. It was universal, and it was local. It was Rome, and it was our parish. It was home, too: the domestic church. In fact, for me, most of the practice and the wonder and the experience of my Catholic faith was in our domestic church, located in a blue, two-story, four-bedroom Cape Cod house at 136 North Lake Shore Drive. My mother taught me my prayers and made sure we children dressed up for Sunday Mass and had a new outfit every year for Easter. Most of the rooms in the house had an image of the Blessed Mother, and on the mantel in the living room stood a revered, refined, elegant statue of the Blessed Mother. It was in the living room, appointed with the finest furniture and a fireplace, that our family would gather after dinner each evening. The lights would be turned low, a candle would be lit, and we would pray the Rosary. My mother would sit on the couch, and my father would kneel up against another couch. Perhaps our family Rosary was in response to Venerable Father Patrick

Peyton's reminder that "the family that prays together stays together." Perhaps it was the good example of Archbishop Fulton Sheen. Whatever the reason, I was aware that most families did not have the custom of praying a daily Rosary together, but we did, and Mom and Dad were completely united in the matter.

But that daily gathering for the family Rosary lasted for only a time. My older brothers and sisters grew up, headed off to college, and started families of their own, and the late 1960s discombobulated venerable family traditions of devotion and prayer. There must have been a five- or six-year lull in the family Rosary, but it came back in 1973, with just three or four of us praying it now, and the intentions were very clear: for our family, for our country, and for the success of my father's brand-new business. The business took off.

I must have been in my twenties and my father in his seventies when I asked him his story about the Rosary. Where did he learn it? Why did he pray it? As the youngest of twelve children growing up on the West Side of Chicago in the Austin neighborhood, he slept out on the front porch, and during the winter he slept in a down sleeping bag. His mother would tuck him in at night, and together they prayed the Rosary. Oh, I thought, so that's how it works: the Rosary, the faith, is passed down personally from generation to generation. I wondered who taught it to my grandmother.

On my mother's side, the Murphy family prayed the Rosary nightly in the living room. Those were the years of the Great Depression and World War II, when the weekly Sorrowful Mother Novena at Our Lady of Sorrows Basilica on the near West Side of Chicago drew ten thousand faithful at a time. Nothing drives the prayer of petition to the Mother of God like the real possibility of losing your sons in action on foreign soil.

I don't know if it was my mother or my father, or both, who told me that they prayed the Rosary daily for each other at 9:00 P.M. during the war. My father was drafted as a buck private in September 1941; four years later he was honorably discharged, having achieved the rank of captain through field promotions and been decorated with the Bronze Star. While my father was in boot camp, the Japanese attacked Pearl Harbor, and five months after that, my parents were married at Fort Lewis, Washington, home of the Forty-First Division—the "Sunset Division"—in the company of a priest and two witnesses, the minimum necessary for a canonically valid marriage. To my knowledge there were no invitations, limousines, showers, or even pictures to celebrate that important occasion; just the mature commitment of two well-formed Catholic youngsters in love, who were willing to pledge their lives to each other and to God and to fulfill the very first commandment given to the human race: "Be fruitful and multiply." By the grace of God and through their mature sense of self-sacrifice, their marriage thrived and lasted for fifty-eight years, until 2000, when my father passed away.

My father rarely spoke about the war years. Later research and reading on my part explained why. The Thirty-Second and Forty-First Divisions reconquered New Guinea and landed at Leyte Gulf with General MacArthur. The casualty rate was extraordinarily high, and life in the jungle was a living hell. More soldiers died of dysentery, beriberi, malaria, jungle rot, and bites from creepy crawlers than from battle wounds. My father knew he was blessed to have survived.

In the spring of 1990, while I was studying in Rome for the priesthood, my folks visited me. One day, we took an excursion down to Nettuno to visit the relics of Saint Maria Goretti. The nearby beaches of Anzio and the perfectly placed little white crosses at the American military cemetery triggered my father's memory, now weakened by age and incipient dementia and too feeble to repress the unpleasant recollections of war. It was then that he explained the events that led to his published poem "Little White Crosses", a pithy and poignant poem worthy of Emily Dickinson.

*Little white crosses,*
*All in a row,*
*The fruit, the Losses,*
*Of seeds we sow.*

*Quaint little plots 'neath*
*Tropical sun,*
*A memory wreath*
*Marks every one.*

*Sad when you reckon*
*The way they fell,*
*Far from the beckon*
*Of home's sweet spell.*

*Stilled is their sleeping,*
*Far from your tears,*
*Quiet your weeping,*
*Banish your fears.*

*What though they slumber*
*'Neath foreign sod,*
*Know they are under,*
*The Hand of God.*

*Sergeant Major Martin A. Hoffman*
*New Guinea, 1943*

One day, on the beach of New Guinea near New Hollandia, enemy shellfire descended upon my father's platoon. Many were wounded, some were killed, and my father, perhaps shielded by a coconut tree, or perhaps with his hand in his pocket holding his rosary and recalling his wife back home praying for him, was left untouched. He did, in fact, credit his safety to the Rosary and the powerful protection of our Blessed Mother. That story made a deep and lasting impression on me. How could it not? A field captain, with extraordinarily strong hands, big muscles, and a quick, calculating mind, found nothing to be ashamed of in his devotion to the Blessed Mother. He did not wear his religion on his sleeve; he did not force it on others; he just lived it. So, on the day Saint John Paul II ordained me a priest for Opus Dei in Rome, my father took me aside on the steps of St. Peter's. As we looked out over the plaza, he placed in my hand the rosary he had carried with him through the war. What a cherished and unforgettable gift, something that I am clearly not worthy to have.

I love the family Rosary. We pray it frequently in Opus Dei centers. It brings people together. It fosters peace and unity. It gives us hope. And it can be very powerful in winning God's decisive grace. That rich, simple, true devotion is a telltale sign that everything is all right in any Church organization: diocese, parish, movement, order, association, prelature, or just a plain old family. And when enough people pray it together for a common cause, it can change the course of history. Saint Pius V knew that well and was able to rally Christians everywhere to pray the Rosary for the safety of Christendom. Those prayers were answered in a miraculous way on October 7, 1517, at the Battle of Lepanto. For that reason, Relevant Radio now offers the Family Rosary across America live on weekdays at 5:00 P.M. (PT), led by Father Dave Heney, pastor of St. Bruno Church in Los Angeles. I think most of the credit for that daily Rosary across America—which reaches 220 million souls in the United States—goes to my father. If he had neglected that daily Rosary, if he had not taken us to weekly Mass, I probably would have followed his example and been one of the many baptized Catholics in our country who lack enthusiasm for our faith.

I don't want to give the wrong impression. We were devout, but our days were never dominated by devotions. Growing up in our family was a lot of fun. Sure, we worked hard and were expected to get good grades, get a part-time job by the time we were fifteen, and go to college. In fact, five of us eight children went on to get doctorates in various fields. But we had lots of fun growing up in the Hoffman Haus. Birthdays, anniversaries, Christmas, and Easter were cause for great celebrations, and backyard barbecues were always the thing for Memorial Day, the Fourth of July, and Labor Day. Family vacations, even on a limited budget, were times for the whole family to be together for a week or two, doing the road trip in a Dodge station wagon with wood paneling on the side and a luggage rack on top. How we squeezed ten Hoffmans into that space, I don't know. But they were very happy times. As we backed out of the driveway, my father—always at the steering wheel—would lead us in a very special and powerful prayer: the Memorare, which we always prayed when we were going on vacations. At the end of the prayer, my father would invoke Our Lady of the Highways, to which we would all respond, "Pray for us." No one questioned it. No one mocked it. No one rolled his eyes. After all, if Jesus is really God, and Mary is His mother and the queen of angels and saints in Heaven, why wouldn't you want her along for the trip to guide and protect you? Years later, I would write a very popular book about the Memorare. I remain convinced of its efficacy. And Relevant Radio has launched the One Hundred Million Memorares for the End to Abortion campaign over our network. My father deserves much of the credit for that prayer reaching millions worldwide as well.

Dad modeled a strong work ethic, entrepreneurial drive, and spirited engagement in discussing the latest in religion and politics. He created an intellectually stimulating atmosphere in our home. We had books everywhere and at least two sets of encyclopedias. While he was probably politically incorrect long before that term existed, he was not afraid to speak the truth, no matter what the consequences were. He had the kind of virility that is rare today, and when it does show up in public life, it is roundly mocked and derided.

So, now you've seen my dad—as I saw him—as a soldier, a businessman, a traveler, a neighbor, a volunteer, a husband, a father, a friend. He was the source of much that I have and almost everything that matters. In wishing such fathers for the next generation, I'm wishing a godly, prosperous, and profoundly happy future.

22

# Father John Riccardo

*Father John Riccardo is a priest of the Archdiocese of Detroit, ordained in 1996. He is currently serving as the executive director of ACTS XXIX, a nonprofit apostolate that exists for the purpose of priestly and Church renewal. Father John served most recently as pastor of Our Lady of Good Counsel in Plymouth, Michigan, where he was witness to the transforming power of the Holy Spirit in a way that caught the attention of pastors across the country. ACTS XXIX works with bishops, priests, and leaders throughout the United States to respond to the urgent call of the past four popes for a new Pentecost and a new evangelization, equipping pastors for the apostolic age in which we live. He hosts the podcast* You Were Born for This *and the radio program* Christ Is the Answer. *He and the ACTS XXIX Team speak at diocesan events across the country. He is a graduate of the University of Michigan, the Gregorian University in Rome, and the Pope John Paul II Institute for Studies on Marriage and the Family. To learn more about ACTS XXIX, please visit www.actsxxix.org.*

"Because of you, honey, I know who God is."

I'll never forget hearing my mother say those words. She said them to my father as he lay in his casket just before my family walked down the main aisle of our parish Church to begin his funeral.

Since then, I've repeated those words countless times to engaged couples preparing to enter into the Sacrament of Marriage. Increasingly so, in my mind, that is *the* point of Marriage. The sacraments are visible signs of invisible realities. But they are special kinds of signs; they cause to happen what they signify. With regard to the Sacrament of Marriage, one way to think about this is to understand that God not only calls a couple to this vocation but also equips them with His grace—that is to say, His supernatural power—to be and to do what He has called them to be and to do. And while there are many ways to understand what they are called to be and to do, a husband is called and equipped to be for his wife, and a wife for her husband, a visible, concrete, tangible sign of God—His love, His kindness, His gentleness, His patience, His mercy, His faithfulness, and so much more.

This, however, is a book about fatherhood, not marriage—though they are clearly intimately connected. So let me come at my father from another angle. Pope Saint John Paul II once wrote, "The mission and the task of fatherhood is to reveal and to relive on earth the very Fatherhood of God." How's that for a task! Just as my mother was able to say to my father's mortal remains, after sixty-six years of marriage, the words I mentioned above, so I was able to say to my father before the Lord called him from this life, "You have given me a glimpse of God, Pop. Because of you, I know God." Indeed, my image of God is profoundly shaped by my earthly father. Every father, in fact, shapes the image—for better or worse—that his children have of God. This is because God *is* Father.

Simply put, my father was the greatest man I have ever known or met—and I lived in the shadow of Pope John Paul II for four years and met him on many occasions. John J. Riccardo was born in 1924 in upstate New York to Italian immigrants who came over from a little town in the south of that country at the end of the nineteenth century. Peter, my grandfather, used to conduct orchestras back in the day when such things were popular. He also held a number of other jobs, including working in a bicycle factory, where he bent handlebars by hand. My dad tried that job for one day and then quit, deciding that higher education was the life for him!

Pop, as I called him, began attending Albany State Teachers College, but his studies were interrupted by World War II. He was drafted and served in Burma and India. Like many men who fought in the war, my dad didn't tell many stories about his time there, except the ones about his friends and their antics that made him laugh. Because of his service in the war, Pop was able to receive a GI scholarship and attended the University of Michigan, where he met my mother. He received his undergraduate degree and master's in economics. In those says, they used to post job interviews on the bulletin board at the business school. My dad put his name on the last vacant slot for Touche Ross, one of the big eight accounting firms at the time. Some months after he started working for the firm, his boss told him that of all the candidates they had interviewed, my dad was by far the least qualified. He was, however, the hungriest, and so they took a chance and hired him. It turned out to be the only interview my dad ever had in his life. From Touche Ross he moved to Chrysler; in 1970, he was named president of the company; and in 1975, he became chairman of the board.

I mention this about his career to set up what I really want to share about my dad. My dad taught me, my older brother, and my three older sisters what a man is. I just recently had a conversation with a good friend, a man less fortunate than I was growing up with regards to fatherhood. He asked me if it would be worthwhile to create a course for young men to teach them about masculinity and manhood. I certainly think so, especially as increasing numbers of young men grow up in homes without a father. My father was that course. A real man, my dad taught us, is one who prays, has faith, entrusts himself to God, reads Scripture, is faithful to the Mass and Confession, pours out his life for his wife, and models the faith for his kids. Because my dad was as successful as he was, it was clear that he didn't need a crutch, as some people ridiculously consider faith to be. The impact of the witness of his faith on me as a young boy and a young man was irreplaceable. I knew by simply watching and listening to him that a life surrendered to the God Who not only created us but also redeemed us by becoming flesh and going to the Cross is not only reasonable but is how a real man should live his life.

Since it is virtually impossible for me to think about my father without thinking also of my mother, I'd like to offer what I have come to call "the seven keys to a thriving marriage" that I learned from them and that I share over and over again with couples.

The first key: build your marriage on self-sacrifice. My mother was not yet Catholic when she married my father, and because of that, they were married at a side altar in the Church of SS. Peter and Paul in Detroit. At the time, 1950, the priest used to share during the wedding ceremony what became known as the Exhortation before Marriage. This was a rather lengthy and downright sober reflection on marriage before the couple exchanged their vows. To my mind, it's the most beautiful reflection on marriage outside of Scripture. For whatever reason, one of the lines in that exhortation stuck in the memories of my mom and dad, and they used to repeat it over and over again to us kids growing up. The line went like this: "Sacrifice [which is the heart of marriage, since it is the heart of love] is usually tedious and irksome. Love can make it bearable, but perfect love makes it a joy." My parents not only repeated those words; they lived them out in front of us. In an age when love is often reduced to a mere feeling, I cannot adequately express how significant it was to learn what love really is by watching my parents' love for each other in action. They enfleshed the words the Church often repeats: "The human person can only find fulfillment by making a sincere gift of self to others" (cf. *Gaudium et spes*, 24).

The second key: anticipate that things will get better. Not easier—better. After my dad died, we found a card he had written to our mom on their sixtieth wedding anniversary. In it, he wrote, "How is it possible that I could love you more today than I did when we walked down the aisle so many, many years ago now? But I do!" We easily get nostalgic in life, looking back and thinking somehow those were the good old days. But the truth of the Christian life is that the best is not in the past; the best is ahead! This is not to say that trials and tribulations will not come; they assuredly will. The details are not important, but it is important to mention that my mom and dad went through a brutal storm shortly after they were married. They could have quit within the first few years. They made a decision, however, to weather the storm and to call out to God for the help only He could give. And He provided. When love gets tested—and all love gets tested—spouses learn not only that they can endure the tests but that they can become stronger through the tests. Spouses learn as well that God's power and faithfulness are real, which then enables a couple increasingly to call on and trust in His provision no matter what comes their way.

The third key: never, ever, ever, keep score. Everybody is competitive, even those who appear to be the gentlest and kindest. Keeping score is for sports, not for love. It is absolutely crucial for a couple to turn their competitive juices into outdoing the other in showing honor and kindness, affection and love.

The fourth key: forgive. Everything. Immediately. No matter what. "As the Lord has forgiven you, so you also must forgive" (Col 3:13). Everyone is in need of constant conversion, so every married person is bound to hurt his spouse. Hopefully, this won't happen intentionally, though it might. But if a husband is to be a sign to his wife of the love of God, can he do so more strikingly than by showing mercy and forgiveness? As painful as it is—and forgiving is always painful—forgiveness can become an extraordinary means of revealing the identity of God to the other and of helping the other to know that, no matter what, God's love is faithful and that He will never abandon us.

The fifth key: if the Lord should bless you with children, remember what children need the most. More than anything else, even more than they need to know that *they* are loved, children need to know that their mom and dad *love each other*. This is one of the many reasons why couples need to make time regularly to go out on dates alone. When kids see their parents enjoying one another and being together, they feel safe. When they do not, kids begin to feel as though everything around them is crashing down.

The sixth key: model the faith for your children. It is often said that, with regard to faith, parents set a kind of "glass ceiling" through which children rarely pass. This is especially true of the impact of fathers on sons. One of the most lasting memories I have of my father is the sight of him kneeling at the foot of his bed every single night before he went to bed. My mom and dad's bedroom was at the end of a long hallway. Before they went to bed, for a while anyway, the door was left open. I don't know if that was intentional or not, but while it was open, I would see my dad on his knees praying. This taught me that a real man prays, and so I began to do what I saw my father do. And then, of course, the door would close for the night.

The seventh key: never forget the point of marriage. Every sacramental marriage is an arranged marriage, for Jesus says, "What therefore God has joined together, let no man put asunder" (Mt 19:6). Why did He arrange this? Simple: so that your wife, or husband, will be able to say to you when you depart from this life, "Because of you, I know God."

My father died on February 13, 2016. As a priest, I had the honor of celebrating his funeral Mass and giving the homily. I would like to share some of my words from that homily that help explain how my father lived the faith and led me to Christ:

"There was a man sent from God whose name was John. He came for testimony to bear witness to the light, that all might believe through him. He was not the Light but came to bear witness to the light." I don't know of a better text to open up my father's life than that one, quite frankly. I don't know how to explain my dad other than to say that he was sent from God and he was and will continue to be, I trust, a remarkable testimony to the light.... Ninety-one years. Any of us could stand here and share lots of stories and memories about our father; he was just that good a man, and he touched us all in remarkably unique ways.

I want to reflect on the topic of greatness as I think about my dad. I have a picture in my bedroom of an occasion when my mother and father and I had a chance to meet Saint John Paul the Great.... I always say that to meet Saint John Paul was to walk away from his presence—without his ever having said anything—as if he had said to you simply these two words: "Be great." It was as if he stood in front of you as a man and said to you, "You don't have anywhere near the gifts that I have, but still you can be great. Just sell it all, give everything for God, and be great." To know my dad and to meet my dad was the same experience. Without his ever having said those words to any of us, his life was simply lived in such a way that it just encouraged us to be great.

My dad had many loves: he loved many people, and he loved many places and things. He loved my mom of sixty-six years more than anybody else on this earth. He loved his children. He loved his grandchildren and his great-grandchildren. He loved all the people in his parish. He loved the people that he served in so many different capacities. He loved the Church. He loved Mexico. He loved Spanish. He loved climbing trees with polesaws: that was his favorite thing to do—even in his eighties! He loved Michigan athletics. But the one my dad really loved was Jesus; my dad lived for Jesus; Jesus was everything to my father.... He was continually living in light of this day, and as soon as he retired, he spent his whole life serving the Church and longing to bring people into an encounter with the one who had so transformed his life, and so I know his prayer today, in a special way, is for those of us who are here who have not yet met him....

I want to look at greatness in light of three Scripture passages that sum up my dad in a very particular way. First is Micah.... It was his favorite Scripture: "Walk humbly with your God" (6:8).... My father dripped humility. Humility doesn't mean that you don't think anything about yourself, or you have an exaggerated low opinion of yourself. Humility means you don't think about yourself. It means you're always thinking of others. It means you're always saying, "Thy will be done, Lord, not mine." And my dad, to our consternation—at least mine when I was growing up—never seemed to think of himself. My dad wore black socks and shorts long before the Fab Five made them famous. He used to wear this floppy little goofy hat which embarrassed us to no end, and a zip-up jacket, white boat shoes, blue ankle-high socks, and shorts—because he thought nothing of himself.... He was in a bank in Mexico one time. We were in Acapulco, where we used to spend our Christmases, and he was in line and talking English, and a gentleman behind him hears him speaking and he says, "Ah, you're from the States. Where ya from?"

"Detroit," my dad says.

"No kidding, I'm from Chicago. What do you do?" the man asks.

"I work in the auto industry."

"Ah, so do I; I'm a supplier. What do you do?"

"Um, I work for Chrysler," my dad says.

"Ah, no kidding, we supply Chrysler! What do you do?"

My dad says, "I'm in management."

The man responds, "Management? What does that mean you're in management?"

My dad says, "I'm in management."

"Come on, what do you do?"

So my dad says, "Well, I'm chief executive officer and chairman of the board."

And the guy stepped back, looked at my dad, and started to laugh.

Saint Paul says in today's second reading, writing to his dear friend Timothy, a spiritual son: "If you would be great, be humble!" Those could easily be my dad's words to all of us, his children, and maybe especially to my mom, that last line: "Do your best to come to me soon." But in that reading, Paul talks about having finished the race. People often say it's all about the journey; no, it's not. It's not about the journey at all; it's about the destination; it's about crossing the finish line, and my dad lived perpetually thinking of the day when he would cross the finish line. My dad was always living in light of this. The ancients always used to say, "Remember death", not out of fear,

but because, if you live life backward, you'll live life better.... The quintessential Christian word, perhaps more
than any other word, is "watch". That's the command
Jesus gives us: Watch. Be alert. Be ready. Don't be scared.
Be ready. My dad was always watching, and because he
was, when the Lord came, he was ready to go. He didn't
need to run to the priest nearby; he was just able to fall
into his grandsons' arms and go home. If you would be
great, then keep the finish line in mind....

Saint John Paul II used to say over and over again
that the mission and the task of fatherhood is to reveal
and relive on earth the Fatherhood of God. He did that
because God is love, and if there is one word to sum up
my dad's life, that word is "love" and specifically "sacrificial love".

How do you walk humbly? How do you keep your
eyes on the finish line? How do you love like Jesus? For
my dad the answer was simple: grace. But not just any
grace—specifically, it was the grace that comes from the
altar. My dad's life was anchored in the Eucharist, not only
on Sundays, but every day. And when Jesus said, "Do
this in memory of me", He meant that you should let
what you receive transform your life. That's the only way
to do this: the only way to love, the only way to live in
humility, the only way to live constantly thinking about
the Lord is to feed on the Lord and to trust yourself to
grace, and my dad did that. This means we can do that if
we want to.

I'll say a special word to my nephews and my nieces
and maybe my grandnephews and grandnieces too, to
share an image that I found to be really helpful. About
three years ago, I was watching a football game. Texas
A&M was playing, and Texas A&M's stadium is known
as the "Twelfth Man". If you don't know anything about
football, I pray you at least know this that there's eleven
players on the field and the twelfth is the crowd, and it's
an extraordinarily obnoxious stadium. Texas A&M is very

loud and doesn't have cheerleaders; instead, they have a drill team whose task it is to whip the crowd into a frenzy. So I'm watching this game between Texas A&M and Nebraska. It's a whiteout, which means the fans are all in white. The game hasn't even started yet—it's just the pregame—and already it's so loud that the stadium is bouncing. And as I'm watching this game, I hear the Lord say to me, "That's Heaven, John", and He took me right to the Letter to the Hebrews, where the author says, "Since therefore we are surrounded by a great cloud of witnesses,... let us run with perseverance the race that is set before us, looking to Jesus" (12:1–2). The image that's used there is the image of athletics. Scripture often uses the image of athletics. Jesus is the greatest athlete. Being an athlete is to compete for a crown. Everybody on earth is competing for a crown.... The saints in Heaven aren't ... looking down at us, saying, "Phew, man, it looks bad, glad that's over for me." They're cheering, and I don't know where dad is yet, I don't know if he's home or if he's on his way, but I can tell you this: when he gets home, if he's not there yet, and he takes his place among those saints, you aren't going to have a bigger cheerleader, especially those of you who sat next to him for so many years. He will be cheering like crazy for you to run the race, to keep the faith, to fight the good fight, to know that as great a friend as he was here, you ain't seen nothing yet. As Saint Thérèse said, "I will spend my life in heaven doing good on earth", and so will he.

23

# The Vander Woudes

*Steven, Daniel, Bob, Chris, Patrick, Joseph, and Father Thomas Vander Woude are the seven sons of Tom and Mary Ellen Vander Woude. Together they have submitted pieces of the story involving their father and their youngest brother, Joseph. Father Thomas is a Catholic priest of the Diocese of Arlington. He graduated from Christendom College, was ordained in 1992, and is the pastor at Holy Trinity Parish in Gainesville, Virginia. Steven is a construction project manager in the Northern Virginia area. He and his wife, Erin (Murphy), have ten children and two grandchildren. They live on "the farm", as it is referred to in this chapter. Steven volunteers as a basketball and soccer coach for his children's teams. Dan is married to Maryan (Lee) and they have seven children. Dan graduated from Christendom College. He has worked in the Catholic education field since graduation and is the basketball coach and athletics director at Seton School. He and his family live on "the farm", where they dabble in hobby farming. Bob and his wife, Melissa (Cooley), are the proud parents of fourteen children (seven boys and seven girls). Bob is a retired Marine Corps aviator—KC130 of twenty years. He graduated from Franciscan University of Steubenville and resides in Simpsonville, Kentucky, where he and his family enjoy hobby farming when he is not flying commercially. Chris is married to Katy (Hadro); they have one daughter, Zelie. Chris graduated from Christendom College and works as an athletics director at a Catholic high school near "the farm" and Katy's family. Patrick and his wife, Jill (Menke), have four children.*

*Patrick is a reserve Marine Corps aviator after serving ten years of active duty. He works as a family nurse practitioner near "the farm", where he and Jill recently built a house. Joseph, the youngest of the brothers, was born in 1987 "on the farm". He has many talents, including tinkering with electronics and calming crying babies, and he loves to golf. He is gifted when it comes to operating equipment and vehicles. He lives with Mom (Mary Ellen) in the farmhouse on "the farm".*

It was September 8, 2008—a normal, beautiful fall day in Northern Virginia. A man was going about his normal daily activities. He had woken up just after sunrise and said his morning prayers before doing a few household chores. This man lived in his dream house. It was an old brick farmhouse built near the turn of the nineteenth century. Something always needed to be fixed or updated—whether it was the water lines freezing in the Virginia winters or the windows with the cement weights getting stuck open.

After the chores, this man would greet two other family members in the house: his beloved wife of forty-three years and their twenty-year-old youngest son, who was blessed with Down syndrome. After the morning chores, it was off to Mass at their local parish, where the man, his wife, and their son were active participants and daily attendees. Since the man had retired, he and his wife hadn't missed a daily Mass. In addition to doing one's daily duties, the man would say that receiving our Lord and Savior is the most important thing that can be done in a day.

Following Mass, it was back to the farm—a modest twenty-six acres with the barns and buildings of what used to be a very large dairy farm. On this day, the task was to get the pool ready for the winter. Together with his youngest son, the man started the work, during which he walked around the house to the side opposite where the pool was.

When he returned to the pool, he noticed something was wrong: his son was nowhere to be found. And the cement top of one of the septic tanks was also missing. The farm had an old septic system with two large cement tanks, each with a two-by-two-foot cement lid with steel handles. These tanks were eight to ten feet deep and about five feet wide. They were connected below the ground to make one very large tank.

The man's son had fallen into the septic tank.

What followed was a demonstration in what it means to be a father. The man yelled to his wife to call 911. Then he immediately jumped into the septic tank. His wife and someone who had been working on the house rushed to the edge of the tank, but they could not reach down far enough to get hold of the young man in there.

"You pull, and I will push," the father said.

Then he took a breath and submerged himself completely in the slop in the tank so he could lift his son above the sewage. While he did this, his wife and the workman tried to grab the son's shirt. But the weight of the sewage on his clothes and the depth of the tank made it impossible for them to pull the son out. So they knelt there at the edge of the large hole in the ground, holding on to the son's clothes, while the man remained underneath until the rescue squad arrived.

When rescue workers arrived, they pulled out the son and his father. The son survived; the father did not. He had been submerged for too long and had suffocated— all the while propping up his son on his shoulders so he could breathe.

This is the story of Thomas S. Vander Woude, our dad, and how he led us to God.

Dad's heroic, life-giving, and final act of service here on earth is both miraculous and inspiring. His story brings tears to the eyes, but also joy to the heart. The beauty of his story is that, as a relative put it, he did the normal things extraordinarily well. The beauty is that we can relate to and, by the grace of God, emulate him. Growing up with Thomas Vander Woude as our father, we were privileged to witness a man on his journey while he encouraged and led us on our own journeys of faith.

Dad led us to God in a variety of ways but especially in how he loved, respected, and treated his wife, the mother of his seven sons; in his hard work and commitment to doing his daily duty; in his unwavering faith in God and trust in His plan; in his tireless service toward those around him; in his simple humility and gentleness; and in his devotion to the Blessed Virgin Mary.

Dad's journey includes potholes, U-turns, crashes, and victories along the way that led him directly to that final act on that sunny fall day in September, when he followed in the footsteps of Our Lord, who said in John 15:13, "Greater love has no man than this, that a man lay down his life for his friends."

There are many stories of Dad's character leading up to that final moment—stories that each of us remembers differently. The overarching theme is that Dad was a man's man. Yet it was never a matter of pompous masculinity, but rather a humble confidence in who he was as a man of God.

This journey had its humble beginnings on a farm outside Sioux Falls, South Dakota, where Dad was an avid athlete. Upon graduation from college, he joined the Navy and flew A-7 Corsairs in Vietnam. If anyone has read or researched much about that war, he knows that the men of that generation had an uncanny sense of courage when literally staring down the barrels of enemy antiaircraft fire.

On the farm, there were always chores and tasks that Dad wanted to complete, some of which turned into summer jobs for us kids during our break from school. From baling hay to cutting horns off steers to breaking stubborn horses, we had the privilege of learning the value of hard work, and sometimes the value of thinking through problems before dashing headlong into them.

One summer day when Patrick was in high school, Dad and Patrick were preparing the hay-baling equipment. Dad was greasing the fitting and didn't pull his arm out in time. The plunging arm caught Dad's arm and momentarily pinched it against the sheet metal of the baler. The top of his wrist sustained a significant laceration. Dad quickly told Patrick to get the van keys and drive him to the emergency room. Patrick felt the need to hurry and sped down the road. But Dad looked over, and with his unique grin—despite winces of pain—he said, "Let's not get into a crash on the way to the hospital." Years later, Patrick remembers this as a lesson in self-restraint. Although it may seem trivial, this episode taught him the importance of maintaining a sense of equilibrium even in the face of pain and discomfort. It taught him to use virtue to insulate himself against the inevitable ups and downs of life.

One spring, Patrick played lacrosse—a sport that at times involves physical clashes between opposing players. Perhaps one of the more unnerving times is when a player is focused on trying to scoop up the ball—while opposing players have the opportunity to apply physical pressure on him. Patrick was in one such situation in a high school game, and out of fear of being contacted by an opposing player, he slinked away from some of the approaching contact. From the sidelines Patrick heard Dad yell, "Don't quit!" This instantly incited Patrick to go from flight to fight. Instead of fighting for the ball, however, Patrick instinctively threw his lacrosse stick at the ground and yelled that he was quitting. The referee instantly flagged Patrick with an unsportsmanlike penalty, and Patrick was sent to the penalty box on the sidelines.

Now, one can imagine how embarrassing this must have been for Dad. Instead of giving Patrick the silent treatment or yelling at him, however, he walked over, patted him on the back, and said he was sorry for yelling. At the time, Patrick was blinded by tears of anger, but after many years of reflection, he began to understand how much this exchange meant to him. For all intents and purposes, my dad would have been justified in admonishing Patrick for such an inappropriate temper tantrum. Instead, he humbled himself to walk over and say he was sorry. This small act showed Patrick that one is never too old or too wise to say he is sorry, even when it is clear that the other person owes the apology.

The day Patrick found out that our dad had died saving my younger brother's life, he was on a U.S. Navy ship in the Caribbean taking part in a humanitarian mission as a Marine helicopter pilot. One of Patrick's buddies on the ship relayed a message for him to call his wife at an unfamiliar number. Patrick went to the ship's pay phone and made the call; the number was for the emergency room— the same emergency room from the hay-baler story. After being told the situation behind his father's death and his younger brother's state in the ICU, Patrick's initial reaction was to grab the rosary from his flight-suit pocket and start to pray. While that may seem like a "normal" thing for a Catholic to do under the circumstances, it was a habit that had been cultivated by our father during those evenings saying the family Rosary. As we can attest, we often did not leave the house for games, or practices, or school dances until we had said the family Rosary. While

Patrick often complied unwillingly, the practice nonetheless became a habit. And so, in that moment of grief, Patrick returned to a prayer that was impressed upon him by
our father.

Dad's unwavering faith in God included a deep love
of the Catholic Church and a tremendous respect for and
devotion to the Blessed Mother. He also had an adventurous spirit that drove him to do high school daredevil
stunts on the snow-covered hills of South Dakota; to land
his A-7 in a snowstorm in Boise, Idaho, just to visit his
brother and sister-in-law; and to run a farm with seven
sons in addition to his full-time job as a pilot. Dad's love
of the faith joined with his adventurous spirit especially in
the many family pilgrimages that Dad and Mom took us
on—or, rather, "forced" us to embark upon.

Three trips stand out.

While living near Atlanta, Georgia, in the late 1970s,
Dad and Mom decided to fly the family to Washington,
D.C., when Pope John Paul II was visiting America.
Though it was almost forty years ago, we will never forget the amazing feeling of seeing the Vicar of Christ in
person, waving to the crowd as his car drove around a
bend in the street. We also remember Dad suggesting that
we hustle to a spot near the road so that we could have a
much better view of the pope in his popemobile. We will
always remember the beaming smile Dad had on his face
in the presence of the pope and how happy he was that his
family was there.

When Pope John Paul II made another trip to the
United States, it was no surprise that Dad and Mom again
decided to take the family to see him. Taking five children
by plane to San Antonio, Texas, from Georgia, however,
must have been full of challenges. Though we were not
able to be close to the Holy Father due to the enormous

size of the crowd, Dad and Mom got us up in the early-morning darkness so that we could get to the site of the papal Mass a few hours before the pope arrived.

The third trip was for World Youth Day in Denver. Father Tom, our oldest brother, and our brother Dan were traveling with a group of teachers, parents, and students by bus to Denver. Dad and Mom took the rest of the family (four younger brothers) by plane and met our group at World Youth Day for the papal Mass. It is a tradition for World Youth Day pilgrims from around the world to sleep outside in the park the night before the papal Mass. Dad and Mom had decided to camp out as well. The weather conditions were extreme. The temperature by day was near 90 degrees, but we woke up around 4:00 A.M. to feel the ice-cold dew soaking through our blankets. Dad took all this in stride and always gave the impression that minor inconveniences were part of the pilgrim spirit. Later that day, we again experienced the incredible joy of being among a million pilgrims from around the world in the presence of the Vicar of Christ. The crowd cheered, "John Paul Two, we love you!" Pope John Paul responded in English over the loudspeaker, "I love you too!" We will never forget seeing my Dad laugh and smile like a boy in the presence of his hero.

Dad has left us with many profound memories. His love for the pope and his faithfulness to the Magisterium have had a lasting impact on us. While in college, Dan was blessed to go with a small group of students and teachers on a short trip to Rome. It was a pilgrimage that greatly strengthened his Catholic faith. The most moving experience of the trip was a personal audience with Pope John Paul II. During the audience, the pope came around to each of those in Dan's group and gave them a personal blessing. Professional pictures of the event were available, so Dan bought a few. Our dad, who worked as an air-line pilot, arranged his schedule just to meet Dan at the airport in New York on his return so he could fly back home with him to Virginia. As he told Dad about the audience with the pope and showed him the pictures, he was deeply moved as Dad welled up with tears. Dad was overjoyed that he was able to pass on his love and admiration for the pope to his son.

Dad's leadership through example was one of his best traits as a father of seven boys. There was nothing that he would ask of us that he wouldn't do himself, from stacking hay in the top of the barn in the heat of July, when temperatures would surpass one hundred degrees, to the mundane task of washing dishes late at night. He had a disciplined personality and never shied away from completing tasks. Such discipline had a tremendous impact on us.

One aspect of Dad's discipline that particularly affected all of us was his devotion to the Eucharist. Every Wednesday, despite busy schedules, Dad and Mom would load us up in the family van and drive nearly an hour to attend a eucharistic holy hour. It was here that we'd see Dad on his knees in adoration. He strengthened this example of eucharistic devotion by spending an additional hour in adoration every week in the middle of the night.

So it was not surprising that one of us answered the call to the priesthood. Our dad was thrilled that one of his boys was a Catholic priest. During the Mass of ordination, tears of joy streamed down Dad's face as he realized that, through the hands of his son, Our Lord would be present in the Eucharist for the faithful.

Though we understood Dad's joy, we were not prepared for the way he congratulated our brother. After Father Tom's first Mass, Dad slowly walked up to him, knelt down in front of him, and said, "Father, may I have your blessing?" This scene of our strong, manly, disciplined father kneeling in humility before his son is an image that we'll never forget. From then on, our older brother was no longer referred to as Tom, but as Father, because if Dad called him that, well, we all had to.

One of the most profound examples Dad gave to his sons—and quite possibly to all those who came in contact with him—was the way he treated women, specifically his wife of countless years and our Blessed Mother. Dad's treatment of our mother undoubtedly came from his relationship and devotion to the Mother of Christ. After four kids and a number of moves across the county due to military assignments—moves that Dad believed were just the price to pay for the important duty of serving one's country—Mom and Dad had a reversion to the Catholic faith and developed a deep devotion to Mary, especially through the family Rosary. We often heard Mom and Dad quote the late Father Patrick Peyton, who famously and truthfully said, "The family that prays together stays together." What this meant practically for our family was that every night we would say the Rosary together. With such a large, wonderful, noisy, crazy family, which now includes more than thirty-five grandchildren, one great-grandchild, and five sisters-in-law, the stories that circulate at family gatherings revolve around many topics, but stories about the family Rosary always seem to surface.

We all have vivid memories of the family gathering in the family room, with one wall covered in pictures of Jesus, Mary, and the saints. Everything was fun and games until Dad started, "In the name of the Father, Son, and Holy Spirit." At that time, Dad would kneel and motion to us older kids, and we would also kneel. One of our family's best memories is the image of our father kneeling, no matter what he had done that day—whether it was running eight miles, rebuilding a tractor engine, chopping a few cords of wood, or baling a few hundred bales of hay. These things never kept Dad from kneeling for the Rosary.

The other woman whom my father loved deeply was our mother. Like Dad's commitment to the Mother of Christ, his commitment to, respect for, and relationship with Mom helped lead us to God. In the Vander Woude house, the quickest and surest way to guarantee some temporary hardship was to say something or do something toward Mom in an inappropriate way. Such behavior was met with "Don't talk to your mother that way!" or "Go to your room until you learn how to talk to your mother" or even just a meaningful glare.

Much can be written about what has been lost in our society with regard to the relationship between husbands and wives, fathers and sons, and mothers and sons. Dad taught all of us a very simple yet important lesson: when a husband loves and respects his wife and demands that their children do the same, the children learn both to respect women and to appreciate the beauty of God's design for the family.

It was Mom who lay there on the edge of that septic tank clinging desperately to the clothes of her youngest son. And it was Mom who—once the emergency workers had arrived—sat on the ground holding her youngest son as they pulled out the lifeless body of her love of more than forty years. Words cannot do justice to the enormous separation that occurred that day—not only of Dad's soul from his body, but of man and woman.

One cannot help but consider Michelangelo's famous statue that stands just inside the majestic St. Peter's Basilica, the *Pietà*. The statue depicts Mary holding the lifeless body of Jesus after He is taken down from the Cross. This image comes to mind whenever we picture Mom holding our little brother after our father had just given his life for his son.

At the public viewing for Dad's body, which took place before his funeral and lasted an entire day, our family was overwhelmed and humbled—not only by the number of people who came but also by what people said about Dad. It usually came down to some version of three things. The first was "The way your father treated your mother and the family, especially your youngest brother, taught me how to be a man, especially a good father and husband." The second: "When I talked with your dad, he just had this smile and way about him that made me feel at peace and seemed as though I was the only one in his world." And finally, "I know your dad died saving your brother, but the truth is that he would have done that for anyone, whether he knew the person or not."

Joseph (or J, as we call him) is the youngest of Dad's seven sons. He was born with Down syndrome. Given the abortion rate for Down syndrome babies (more than 90 percent), Dad's sacrifice couldn't have stood in further contrast to the ways of the world.

Dad and Mom poured their hearts and souls into Joseph. Because of Down syndrome, Joseph was delayed in most things he did (except playing golf, tech troubleshooting, and driving vehicles)—including walking and crawling. So Dad and Mom would put on rollerblading elbow and knee pads and crawl around the house with Joseph to get him to practice creeping and crawling.

The world says that persons with Down syndrome live less than full lives. This couldn't be further from the truth. Joseph—like most people with this condition—is, in many ways, how all people should be. First, he is happy. Second, persons with Down syndrome have no prejudices; they

love everyone—in a very real and simple way! Not only
is Joseph loving, but he has called our entire family to a
higher level of sacrifice, humility, and love, which, when
last I checked, was a good thing—especially for a family
with seven boys!

While Dad was still flying for the airlines, Mom taught
and nurtured Joseph. When Dad retired, it was his turn to
spend time with his youngest son. They went golfing
together. Joseph is a natural golfer, while Dad had golfed
only a few times before he started golfing with Joseph.
But Joseph liked it, so Dad went with him. When Dad
took a part-time job at a college, Joseph went along with
him. When Dad coached the team, Joseph went on the
trips with them. All of the guys counted him as part
of the team. During time-outs, Joseph would go shoot
free throws—much to the enjoyment of the fans, no matter which side they were on! In all of this, Dad and Mom
never, ever allowed anyone to treat Joseph differently or as
if he were "below" anyone else. Seeing this love, affection,
commitment, and generosity from our parents encouraged
us brothers to treat Joseph the same way.

There is a certain fittingness to the fact that Dad gave his
last breath on this earth to save the son whom he had spent
the most time with and who had brought so much love
to the family. Joseph was born in the farmhouse and his
first moments on Earth were in the hands of his father.
Twenty years later, just a few feet away, he would once
again be "born again" by the hands of Dad when he was
saved from certain death. That day in September, Dad
gave Joseph more life through his hands, and, in return,
he received birth into eternal happiness with God and all
the saints!

Dad poured himself out, day in and day out, throughout his life. It should be no surprise that his last act on this

earth was the crowning glory of a life lived in service. We witnessed the journey that God destined for Dad. He led us in so many ways while he walked this earth. We know by faith that he still leads us, possibly in even more ways than before. Dad led us by his joy and charity. The joy of his simple smile could put the most stressed person at ease. His charity time and again revealed how we are to treat everyone by serving them. He led us to God by his example. It's an example that impacted lives even without words being spoken. He led us to God by showing us what our loving Father is like.

He led us to God in his life. He leads us to God through his death.

# CONCLUSION

For several years I have stood on the sidewalk outside the Planned Parenthood in Providence to pray and talk to the women entering the building. Two years ago, I was able to strike up a conversation with a young man named Dan whose girlfriend was inside having a surgical abortion performed on their son or daughter. Dan did not deny the humanity of his baby or the fact that it was his baby. He simply repeated the modern mantra that our society taught him so well: "It's her choice." According to Dan, there was nothing he could do, or should do, to protect his child. After going a few rounds with Dan and trying to open his mind to the gravity of what was about to happen and explaining that he did, in fact, have a natural, if not legal, right to protect his child, I watched him walk away. He flicked his cigarette to the ground, shrugged his shoulders, and repeated for the last time, "Thanks, man, but there's nothing I can do." Imagine thinking as a father that you have no say in your child's scheduled execution.

I was dumbfounded. I paced the sidewalk, trying to understand how a grown man could be so callous about the life he created. Many times, the boyfriend will say there is nothing he can do, but you can tell it's merely his cowardly way of washing his hands of the responsibility of a baby he doesn't want with a woman he doesn't love. Dan was different. Dan really cared for the woman inside. He seemed content, if not happy, about the prospect of having a child. And yet he truly believed that he had no moral standing in the life or death of his child.

I bring up my encounter with Dan because I see it as an appropriate metaphor for modern Catholic fatherhood and our failure to protect our children. We have been tricked. Fooled. Duped. We have been overpowered and undermined by other people too, of course, but the tide of fatherhood could only have been turned so forcefully and suddenly by demonic activity. Satan aimed right for the heart of God's plan—fatherhood, that awesome vocation of spiritual might and influence—and neutered it. Entrusted with the duty and power to create life and mold children's minds, fathers today no longer believe they even have a say in whether their babies live or die. And if they have no *choice* over the life and death of their children in the womb, why should they feel a special obligation to lead, protect, and educate them once they are born? It is as though God gave us a mighty sword to wield, and we have laid it down or, worse, given it away to men and women who use it to destroy our children—sometimes literally, as in the case of abortion.

There is a curious line in a popular Catholic prayer called "Hail Holy Queen". In the opening lines of the prayer, we turn to Mary and entrust our care to her eternal queenship, but then we hear these unexpected words: "To thee do we send up our sighs, mourning and weeping in this valley of tears." Here the Church describes this life given to us by an all-loving God as a valley of tears, one of the saddest images the mind can conjure. One might expect a happier depiction from the religion that proclaims "good news". Yet this is one of the pivotal and timeless messages of the Church. During our lives, we cannot escape the reality of sorrow, because we are, as the prayer indicates, "poor banished children of Eve", which is to say that we are impacted by sin. We sin, and the people around us sin, and this inevitably leads to sadness. This is a reason God revealed Himself through Jesus Christ. God became man and suffered, in order to wipe away our tears, and in fact, to turn our tears into opportunities for grace. We have a God Who has entered into human pain and, more amazingly, has emptied death, the ultimate sadness, of its heartache and sting, by offering to every person eternal happiness in His presence. Fathers, would you really keep such joy and hope from your children? Will you really abandon them to cry on the shoulder of the modern world? We have seen for several decades the spoiled fruits of taking our children away from Christ and handing them over to the religions of secularism, materialism, and nihilism. It is time, fathers, to share the good news of Jesus Christ with your children and bring them back to God.

I thank God for having given me a father and mother, James and Deborah Rowley, who rightly ordered my mind to love God above all things. I am fortunate and indeed blessed to have their witness of marriage and devotion to the one true faith. My family's commitment to the Church has grown considerably since we were children, motivated in large part by our youngest brother's ordination to the priesthood, but in no small part due also to the consistent witness of a committed father who got on his knees each Sunday in front of his four sons. Without a weekly reminder of the strength and transcendence of God, it is likely our religious commitment would be significantly different today. My brothers and I are all intentional Catholics today because of our father.

That brings to mind one final group of people who need to be addressed: those who do not have a positive fatherly witness to lead them to Christ. How can these men and women come to know and love the gospel? First, they ought to recognize that their worldview likely depends on the life and example of their fathers, for better or for worse. This realization will enable them to consider other viewpoints and hopefully to begin to contemplate the claims of Christianity. We have admitted that Catholicism is not true simply because of a father's Catholic witness, but by the same token, we should also readily affirm that Catholicism is not *false* simply because of the lack of a father's witness. Each person should investigate the claims of the Church on their own merits. This is what the Church asks of each person: to ask, seek, knock. God's grace, we believe, will answer you and open your mind to His love, which, when experienced, will consume you and change you forever. Then you will see that all along, it was not He who was hiding, but you.

At the same time, Catholic men need to be hyperaware of how many young people have no good fatherly examples, and they need to stand as ready witnesses. Coaches, neighbors, godparents, mentors, teachers, and friends need to seize opportunities to be living witnesses of Christ and Saint Joseph. Grounded in prayer, these men need to be ready to step up to the plate in a host of situations, "refathering" the scattered flock one lamb at a time.

The world will be reordered and saved through the gospel. I believe this battle will be led by the kinds of fathers described in this book, but it will take legions more of them to win. May all men take up their crosses and wield the sword of fatherhood to lead, protect, and educate the souls entrusted to them by God, our Father.